ONE LIFE

ONE LIFE THAT

CHANGES EVERYTHING

FOR EVERYONE

PHIL MOORE

MONARCH
BOOKS

Oxford, UK & Grand Rapids, USA

Published by Monarch Books
an imprint of
Lion Hudson IP Ltd
Wilkinson House, Jordan Hill Road,
Oxford OX2 8DR, England
Email: monarch@lionhudson.com
www.lionhudson.com/monarch

ISBN 978 0 85721 801 8
e-ISBN 978 0 85721 802 5

First edition 2017

Acknowledgments
Unless otherwise indicated, Scripture quotations taken from the
Holy Bible, New International Version Anglicised. Copyright © 1979,
1984, 2011 Biblica, formerly International Bible Society. Used by
permission of Hodder & Stoughton Ltd, an Hachette UK company.
All rights reserved. "NIV" is a registered trademark of Biblica. UK
trademark number 1448790.
Scripture quotations marked The Message taken from The
Message. Copyright © by Eugene H. Peterson 1993, 1994, 1995,
1996, 2000, 2001, 2002. Used by permission of NavPress Publishing
Group.

A catalogue record for this book is available from the British
Library

Printed and bound in Great Britain by
Marston Book Services Ltd, Oxfordshire

Contents

Introduction: One Life

There are a lot of people in the world. Seven and a half billion of them, and that number is rising fast. It doesn't matter how much the adverts on TV try to convince us that we are unique, it's easy to feel very small, one solitary life lost in the middle of a vast crowd.

When we look back on history, we feel even smaller. Historians tell us that there are as many people alive today as have lived in all previous generations put together. That makes you one in 15 billion or more, a tiny dot on the landscape of humanity. It's no wonder that so many people feel insignificant. Emma Stone could be talking to any of us when she confronts Michael Keaton in the movie *Birdman* and points out that he's scared his life doesn't matter – *You're right, your life isn't important. Neither are you, so get used to it!*

But I have written this book because I have good news for you: Emma Stone is wrong. Your life is important. You are significant. Not because of who you are, but because of who somebody else is and because of what that person says about you and what he has done for you. I have written this book to explain how one person's life has changed everything for your own. It isn't a long book, but if you read it slowly and thoughtfully it will transform the way you live and love and laugh and hope and play and work and die. I know that for a fact, because the things I'm going to tell you are already transforming my own life and the lives of some of the friends that I'm going to introduce to you in these pages. I'm going to invite you to join us on our journey of discovery.

I'm going to tell you about the life of one solitary soul in the midst of 15 billion. He did none of the things that normally lead to greatness yet he is by far the most thought about, talked about, written about, sung about, blogged about and tweeted about person in history. His immense significance is undeniable and it isn't just theoretical. He claimed that everything he said and did was intended to transform the lives of people like you and me. There's a famous saying about him:

He was born in an obscure village, the child of a
peasant woman. He grew up in another obscure
village. He worked in a carpenter's shop until
he was thirty, and then for three years he was
an itinerant preacher. He never owned a home.
He never wrote a book. He never held an office.
He never had a family. He never went to college.
He never put his foot inside a big city. He never
travelled two hundred miles from the place where
he was born. He never did any of the things that

*one usually associates with greatness. He had no
credentials but himself.*

*While still a young man, the tide of popular
opinion turned against him. His friends ran away.
One of them denied him. He was turned over to his
enemies. He went through the mockery of a trial.
He was nailed to a cross between two thieves. While
he was dying his executioners gambled for the only
piece of property he had on earth – his coat. When he
was dead, he was laid in a borrowed grave through
the pity of a friend. Twenty centuries have come and
gone, and today he is the central figure of the human
race and the leader of human progress. All the armies
that have ever marched, all the navies that have ever
sailed, all the parliaments that have ever sat and
all the kings that have ever reigned, put together,
have not affected the life of humans on this earth as
powerfully as that one solitary life.*

How did an obscure Galilean named Jesus of Nazareth
manage to split the whole of history into BC and AD,
dividing history into events before and after his birth?
How did he punctuate our calendar with the great
festivals of *Christmas* and *Easter*, both of which are
celebrations of what he did for us? More to the point,
why are those events so important for you and me
today? Why do people describe the One Life of Jesus
as the *Good News*? This short book answers all those
questions and many more.

I have divided the book into six parts. Each one

explores a major aspect of the life of Jesus. I begin each part with the basic facts, explaining what Jesus said and did. Then I get very practical by introducing you to somebody who explains how these facts have transformed their own life today. I finish each part with some critical analysis, asking what evidence we have to believe that these facts are really true.

I hope to help you to grasp what eludes the many people who allow the face of Jesus of Nazareth to get lost in the crowd. I hope to help you to understand what Napoleon Bonaparte only realized in his dying days in exile on the island of St Helena. His own life spent, he turned to his old friend General Montholon and confessed that

> *Alexander, Caesar, Charlemagne and I have founded empires. But upon what did we rest the creations of our genius? Upon force! Jesus Christ alone founded his empire upon love; and at this moment millions of men would die for him. I die before my time, and my body will be given back to earth, to become food for worms. Such is the fate of him who has been called the Great Napoleon. What an abyss between my deep misery and the eternal kingdom of Christ, which is proclaimed, loved, and adored, and which is extended over the whole earth! Call you this dying? Is it not living, rather?*[1]

So let's set out on a journey of discovery. Let's explore

1   Quoted by John Abbott in his classic biography *The Life of Napoleon Bonaparte* (1860).

the facts about the greatest man who has ever lived. You have only got one life to live, so it's only right you want to live it to the full. Let's discover the One Life that changes everything for everyone.

PART 1

He Became Flesh

He Became Flesh

Whichever way you look at it, Christmas is a very odd time of year. We give presents that are not wanted (one in every three gifts, if you believe the surveys) to people that we don't get on with (the average family begins to argue by 9:58 on Christmas morning), while eating party food that tastes so unpleasant we avoid it for the rest of the year (don't even get me started on Brussels sprouts). But weirder than all of this is the fact that most of our celebrations ignore the meaning of the party. A study of the 1,739 Christmas cards on sale in Tesco, the largest retailer in Britain, found that only seven of them depicted the birth of Jesus. It's as if we have forgotten what made our ancestors so excited when they made Christmas the greatest festival of the year.

Our journey of discovery therefore starts with good news. Christmas was meant to be more than binge-eating and TV-watching. It was never meant to be an excuse for big businesses to raid your pockets once a year. Lost amid the wrapping paper on the floor and drowned out by Michael Bublé crooning "Santa Claus Is Coming to Town" is a message that has inspired millions of people for 2,000 years. I love the way that an early scholar of the life of Jesus we are studying sums up the true meaning of Christmas: *"He became what he was not so that we might become what he is."*

He became what he was not. It's crucial that we understand this if we want to grasp the true significance of Jesus of Nazareth.

One of the twelve original disciples of Jesus was a man named John, who wrote a famous record of his life and teaching. He emphasizes several times that Christmas was not the start of the story for Jesus, but merely the start of his story as a man. He tells us that Jesus talked about *"the glory I had with you before the world began"* and that he claimed to be the God who had created the whole universe. He recalls that Jesus looked back to the founding father of the Jewish nation, who lived 2,000 years before his birth, and declared that *"Before Abraham was born, I am!"* When John and his friends started worshipping Jesus as *"My Lord and my God!"*, instead of correcting them he commended them and asked them why it had taken them so long to understand.[1] This is the amazing truth that lies at the heart of our Christmas celebrations. The God who created the universe became part of the universe he had created. He became a baby in a manger in a dirty stable in Bethlehem, a small town in first-century Israel. God became what he was not so that we might become what he is.

---

1   You can find John's gospel in the Bible. See John 1:1–15; 8:56–58; 12:41; 17:5; 20:28–29.

In order to explain the birth of Jesus, John introduces us to the concept of the Trinity – the idea that God exists in three distinct persons: Father, Son and Spirit. Some of the greatest human minds have grappled with this concept for the past 2,000 years, trying to explain how God can be both one and three at the same time. The fact that they have not fully succeeded shouldn't surprise us. I have a pet catfish that watches all that happens in my family from its fish tank, but I don't expect it to understand my family. We're too complex for its fishy brain to fathom, just as God is too complex to be pinned down by the limited capacity of our human minds. John simply tells us that Jesus is the Word of God, the second Person of the Trinity:

> *In the beginning was the Word, and the Word was*
> *with God, and the Word was God. He was with*
> *God in the beginning. Through him all things were*
> *made; without him nothing was made that has*
> *been made… The Word became flesh and made his*
> *dwelling among us. We have seen his glory, the*
> *glory of the one and only Son, who came from the*
> *Father, full of grace and truth.*

John and the other early historians of the life of Jesus don't just emphasize his divinity. They also emphasize his humanity. They tell us that Jesus grew tired and hungry and thirsty. He loved and laughed and told stories. He was troubled and moved to tears and devoted to his mother.[2] His birth as a human baby

2   See John 4:6; 11:33–36; 12:27; 13:21; 19:25–28. See also Matthew 4:2 and

in Bethlehem did not make Jesus anything less than God but nor did his divinity make him anything less than human. He became fully one of us, as the early theologian Augustine of Hippo explains:

> *The Maker of man was made man, that the Ruler of the stars might suck at the breast; that the Bread might hunger, that the Fountain might thirst, that the Light might sleep, that the Way might be wearied by the journey, that the Truth might be accused by false witnesses, that the Judge of the living and the dead might be judged by a mortal judge, that Justice might be condemned by the unjust, that the Chastener might be chastened with whips, that the Vine might be crowned with thorns, that the Foundation might be hung on a tree, that Strength might be made weak, that Health might be wounded, that Life might die. He suffered these and many other indignities for us, so that he might free us who are unworthy.*[3]

Read Augustine's words again a bit more slowly. They are seriously good news. We live on a fairly small planet in a relatively small solar system. Our sun is one of 200 billion stars in the Milky Way, and astronomers tell us that the Milky Way is one of over 500 billion galaxies in the known universe. It's no wonder we feel small! Carl Sagan sums up our culture's view of what

Luke 10:21. The disciples of Jesus emphasize his humanity because only by becoming fully human was he able to fully save humans.

3   Augustine of Hippo in c. 400 AD in a sermon "On the Birth of Our Lord" (*Sermons* 191.1).

this means for us in his book *Cosmos*, concluding that

> *We float like a mote of dust in the morning sky…*
> *We live on an insignificant planet of a hum-drum*
> *star lost in a galaxy tucked away in some forgotten*
> *corner of a universe in which there are far more*
> *galaxies than people… The universe seems neither*
> *benign nor hostile, merely indifferent to the*
> *concerns of such puny creatures as we are.*[4]

The Incarnation of Jesus – the fact that God has become a human being – is therefore brilliant news. It announces that Carl Sagan's depressing verdict on the universe is wrong. We may live on a minor planet that revolves around a minor star in a minor galaxy, but the whole purpose of the universe revolves around us. God has not become a Martian. He has not become a Klingon or a Wookie. He became a man because he made the human race in his own image and because he loves us more than any other creature in the universe he has made. That's the tragedy when we allow the tinsel and the turkey to become the main event at Christmas. We end up short-changing ourselves.

The real meaning of Christmas is great news, but it's also very sobering. When the cavalry arrive in an old Western movie, it's always because the cowboys are in trouble. When Superman flies onto the screen, it's always because somebody is in danger and in desperate need of rescue. With Christmas, it's just the same. The first time in the Bible that God promises to

4   Carl Sagan in *Cosmos* (1980).

come to earth as a human being is in Genesis 3:15, just a few verses after the first humans have sinned and messed up the universe that they were given. The rest of the Bible continues on a similar theme. It is because of our failure to live as we ought that God has become a human being, to succeed wherever we have failed.

The Bible uses a technical word to describe humanity's moral failure. The word is taken from the language of an ancient bowman on the shooting range. *Sin* referred originally to an arrow missing the target, so the Bible uses it to describe the many ways in which our own lives miss the target of living rightly towards God and towards those around us. *"For all have sinned and fall short of the glory of God,"* the Bible explains, but *"God made him who had no sin to be sin for us, so that in him we might become the righteousness of God."* One man messed up and we have all messed up by following in his footsteps, so God became a new and perfect man for us to follow instead. *"Since death came through a man, the resurrection of the dead comes also through a man. For as in Adam all die, so in Christ all will be made alive."*[5]

It may not sound like good news to be told that you're a sinner, but it really is. It gives us somewhere to go with the uneasy sense we all have within our consciences, whenever we are honest with ourselves, that we haven't lived as perfectly as we ought to have done. It tells us that God knows all about our sin yet has not given up on us. He still loves us and he has

---

5   The apostle Paul in the Bible. See Romans 3:23; 1 Corinthians 15:21–22; 2 Corinthians 5:21.

proved it to us by coming to earth to live as one of us. He has stooped down to sit in the dust of our planet with us in order to take us up into the glories of heaven with him. We should all want this to be true. If what we celebrate each Christmas is that God loves us so much that he has become one of us in order to forgive us our sins and to lead us back onto the pathway that leads to life and immortality with him, then it's a Happy Christmas indeed.

It gets even better. When Jesus ascended back to heaven at the end of his earthly life, he did not take off his humanity like an unwanted Christmas sweater. He clung on to it. He is still fully human. There is a flesh-and-blood man seated right now in heaven, just as the Bible declares:

> *"This is good, and pleases God our Saviour, who wants all people to be saved and to come to a knowledge of the truth. For there is one God and one mediator between God and mankind, **the man Christ Jesus**, who gave himself as a ransom for all people."*[6]

God became a human being forever so that we can be united with him forever. It's no wonder that previous generations inaugurated the world's biggest party to celebrate such good news.

One of the most successful Christmas movies of all time is *Love Actually*. It begins and ends with countless people hugging and kissing one another in the arrivals

6   The apostle Paul says this in 1 Timothy 2:3–6.

lounge at London's Heathrow Airport as the Christmas holidays begin. Enjoy the movie, but don't miss the fact that Christmas is about something even greater. It celebrates the moment when God embraced the human race by becoming one of us. It celebrates the fact that this means we are not meaningless life forms stuck on a meaningless rock that orbits a meaningless ball of fire in a meaningless universe. We are the only life form in the universe that God loved enough to come and kiss in person that very first Christmastime.

John 3:16–17 explains the reason for our Christmas parties: *"God so loved the world that he gave his one and only Son, that whoever believes in him shall not perish but have eternal life. For God did not send his Son into the world to condemn the world, but to save the world through him."*

Julia's Story

Julia is one of my friends from Everyday Church in London

As a child, my mum and I meant the world to one another. However, as she had been criticized by others, she in turn criticized me. From an early age my sense of significance came from battling to gain her approval.

I tried so hard as a child, but as a teenager I felt suffocated. I never felt good enough, so I looked for love in a chain of boyfriends. Each relationship ended when my intensity scared them away, and my relationship with my mum became more and more strained. When one of my boyfriends proposed, my mum said he wasn't right for me, so I stormed out and moved in with him. In my heart of hearts, I knew that my fiancé was not right for me. I knew he wouldn't fill the hole I had in my life or give me the significance and true worth that I longed for. But I felt it was the only hope I had.

Wonderfully, my mum had come to know God a few months earlier. The night I left home she lay in her bedroom, in the dark and in despair. Suddenly she saw a bright light on her shoulder. She felt God speak to her personally and comfort her that he would look after me and turn the situation around for good.

Over the next two years, I watched the changes that knowing God was making to my mum. I couldn't get over what I saw. She had been depressed for years but was now so full of childlike joy that even my dad, who had been an atheist for years, started reading about Jesus and came to know God too. Then his life began to change as well. Their turbulent marriage was unrecognizable. I couldn't get my head around the beautiful changes that I now saw – in both of them!

I was now at university and engaged to a new fiancé. I decided to go with my parents to church during the holidays, just to see what had changed them so much. Each time I entered the church, I started to cry. I felt struck to the core by a beautiful love I had never experienced before. I knew I wanted more. The sermons I heard at the church told me that I could know God for myself, but I hesitated. If I stopped sleeping with my fiancé, I knew that I would lose him.

So much of my security and self-worth was pinned on him that I didn't feel strong enough to take that loss.

But God amazingly reached down into my situation. My fiancé phoned to say, *"I'm leaving you"* and then hung up on me. To this day I don't know why he did it! I cried for a week but then I suddenly realized that there was nothing holding me back any more. I finally understood that no amount of love from my mum or from my boyfriends could ever make me whole. I asked Jesus to forgive me and I thanked him for coming to earth to get me. I asked him to be my Lord and the best friend that I'd been searching for.

From that day on, God began to reveal his love to me as my Father. He showed me how much he sings in his delight over me. The value of something is shown in how much someone is willing to pay for it. When God showed me that he was willing to spend the life of his own Son on me, I suddenly realized my incredible value to him. I felt him say that he wanted to give me two new names: *"Precious Daughter"* and *"Beautiful as the Sun"*. Discovering how much God loves me has reshaped my whole identity.

I had suffered from depression and I remember the exact place I was standing when God took it away. I had also suffered from panic attacks. These were healed more gradually, but they went away too. Over the next few years, God transformed the way I thought, in every area of my life. He also began to heal my relationship with my mum. We forgave each other. Today I receive the most incredible love, care and support from my mum, which is a true delight.

Most significantly, God transformed my relationships. I now have a wonderful husband. He is calm, consistent and an amazingly strong character. He is just right for me and I thank God so much for him – but my value, identity and joy do not come from him. They come from being loved by the God of the universe, who came to get me. My security comes from knowing that God is my Dad and that he is always smiling at me. He loves me when I'm bad and he loves me when I am good. He loves me all the time. He came from heaven to get me and he will never leave me.

If you feel like I felt, searching for your true identity and worth, then you need to discover the One Life of Jesus like I did. God loves you so much that he came in person to get you. All you need to do is to say yes to him.

Too Good to Be True?

I like talking to people about what they believe. I find it fascinating that each one of us is so different. We are all shaped by what our parents taught us, by what the culture all around us says is true and by what we want to believe ourselves.

Even though the news that God has become one of us ought to be received as the best news that ever fell on human ears, I find it fascinating that so many people never give it a second thought. I remember chatting with an educated businesswoman who told me she believed that Jesus never existed, when even a cursory look at the history books would have shown her that his birth in Bethlehem is undeniable.

The Romans executed Jesus and threw his followers to the lions. The Roman historian Tacitus despises Christianity as one of the *"degraded and shameful practices"* that flourished in Rome, yet even he admits that Jesus was a real man in history. After the Great Fire of Rome, he tells us that

> *Nero fastened the guilt [for the Great Fire of Rome] and inflicted the most exquisite tortures on a class*

hated for their abominations, called Christians by
the populace. Christ, from whom the name had
its origin, had suffered the death-penalty during
the reign of Tiberius at the hands of one of our
procurators, Pontius Pilate, and a most mischievous
superstition, thus checked for the moment, again
broke out not only in Judea, where the evil began,
but even in Rome.[1]

The Jews had persuaded the Romans to execute him and they did all they could to eradicate the Christian faith too. Yet even they did not attempt to deny the life of Jesus. The facts were simply too well documented. Josephus, the greatest Jewish historian of the first century, feels he has no choice but to record that

There was about this time, Jesus, a wise man, if it
be lawful to call him a man, for he was a performer
of wonderful miracles – a teacher of such men as
receive the truth with pleasure. He drew over to him
both many of the Jews and many of the Gentiles. He
was the Christ, and when Pilate, at the suggestion
of the principal men among us, condemned him to
be crucified, those that loved him at first did not
forsake him, for he appeared to them alive again the
third day.[2]

Naturally, the first-century Christian historians give us greater detail about the life of Jesus. They record

1   Tacitus wrote this in c. 110 AD in his *Annals of Imperial Rome* (15.44).
2   Flavius Josephus wrote this in c. 93 AD in his *Antiquities of the Jews* (18.3.3).

his teaching, which even unbelievers throughout history have had to concede is pretty compelling. It's hard to disagree with his commands to *"Do to others what you would have them do to you"* and to *"Love your neighbour as yourself"*.[3] The early Christians record his kindness towards little children, tax collectors and dirty prostitutes – after all, when God stoops down from heaven to become a human it isn't much more of a journey to extend love even to the lowest of the low. The early Christians record his miracles, which his enemies attribute to magic but never try to deny. They also tell us that he did something only God can do. He went around forgiving people for their sins.

C. S. Lewis, the author of the Narnia novels, said that this was one of the most compelling proofs to him that, in Jesus of Nazareth, God had truly become a human being:

> *What this man said was, quite simply, the most shocking thing that has ever been uttered by human lips... I mean the claim to forgive sins: any sins. Now unless the speaker is God, this is really so preposterous as to be comic. We can all understand how a man forgives offences against himself. You tread on my toe and I forgive you, you steal my money and I forgive you. But what should we make of a man, himself unrobbed and untrodden on, who announced that he forgave you for treading on*

3   Matthew 7:12; 22:39. If you have never read Matthew's gospel in the Bible, I recommend it to you. It will only take you two hours to read and it gives a simply stunning insight into the One Life that changes everything.

other men's toes and stealing other men's money?
Asinine fatuity is the kindest description we should
give of his conduct. Yet this is what Jesus did. He
told people that their sins were forgiven, and never
waited to consult all the other people whom their
sins had undoubtedly injured. He unhesitatingly
behaved as if He was the party chiefly concerned,
the person chiefly offended in all offences. This
makes sense only if He really was the God whose
laws are broken and whose love is wounded in every
sin. In the mouth of any speaker who is not God,
these words would imply what I can only regard
as silliness and conceit unrivalled by any other
character in history…

A man who was merely a man and said the sort of
things Jesus said would not be a great moral teacher.
He would either be a lunatic – on a level with the man
who says he is a poached egg – or he would be the
Devil of Hell. You must make your choice. Either this
man was, and is, the Son of God: or else a madman
or something worse. You can shut Him up for a fool,
you can spit at Him and kill Him as a demon; or you
can fall at His feet and call Him Lord and God. But
let us not come with any patronising nonsense about
His being a great human teacher. He has not left that
open to us. He did not intend to.[4]

Not only is this good news, but it is also true. His
friends and his enemies bear testimony to him. God

4   C. S. Lewis in his classic book *Mere Christianity* (1952).

has become a human being. Now he calls you to believe that One Life has changed everything for everyone, and that everyone means you.

PART 2

He Lived Among Us

He Lived Among Us

I don't know if you got caught up in a hashtag that trended recently on Twitter. I'm talking about #ExplainAFilmPlotBadly. Let's see if you can recognize the film described here: "Rural youth is radicalized by religious leader and kills thousands in high-profile bombing." That's kind of what happens in *Star Wars*, but at the same time it isn't at all.

Let's try another one: "Transported to a surreal landscape, a young girl kills the first person she meets, then teams up with three strangers to kill again." That's Dorothy in *The Wizard of Oz*. "A mysterious loner uses the promise of free sweets to lure five children into a secluded warehouse." That's *Charlie and the Chocolate Factory*. Let's try one last film: "Teenage girl volunteers to kill children in public in order to cheer up her younger sister." Yes, that's Katniss Everdeen in *The Hunger Games*. Even if you weren't caught up in the hashtag, you get the general idea. All those plot summaries are valid, yet they are also entirely misleading.

Many people make the same mistake when they consider the life of Jesus of Nazareth. Even those who talk about his birth at Christmas time and his death on Good Friday tend to have a rather sketchy view of what happened in between. The most popular creed that is recited by Christians in churches today tells us that Jesus *"was conceived by the Holy Spirit, born of the Virgin Mary, suffered under Pontius Pilate, was crucified, died and was buried; he descended to the dead. On the third day he rose again; he ascended into heaven and is seated at the right hand of the Father; he will come again to judge the living and the dead."*[1] Did you notice the way that it leaps straight from his birth to his death? I don't want to criticize a creed that has been recited in churches for getting on for 2,000 years, but shouldn't a summary of the life of Jesus – how can I put it? – actually mention his life? I'm thinking of starting my own hashtag. How about #ExplainOneLifeBadly?

Although it goes unmentioned in the creed, after his birth Jesus grew up as a child. The early chapters of Luke's gospel make much of the fact that he was passionate for God and completely obedient to his parents, even at a very early age. Jesus then became a teenager. He had to deal with puberty and hormones and mood swings and homework. Jesus reached his twenties, when he had to handle the death of Joseph, working as a carpenter to put bread on the table for his widowed mother and his fatherless brothers and sisters. He dealt with the challenge of singleness as all his friends paired off and married, leaving him as

1   Written in the fourth century and still recited across the world today, this is known as The Apostles' Creed.

almost the only single guy his own age in the village. When he became a high-profile public figure, he had to learn to handle the challenges of fame and fortune and flattery. Unless we explore these things that happened in the years between Jesus' birth and his death, we will miss out on what his One Life means for our own.

Matthew, Mark, Luke and John place great importance on the events of Jesus' life, and not just on his birth and his death. They tell us that his major teaching method was to invite a select group of students to leave everything behind in order to live their lives with him. He wanted them to observe his sinless life at first hand, so that they could treat it as a model for them to follow. More than that, he wanted them to witness the perfection of his own lifestyle to give them faith that God would forgive all their sins.

A few years ago, my wife and I received a visit from a friend named Caroline. She wasn't a believer in Jesus, but she became curious after seeing something I posted on Facebook about him. She came round unannounced to find out if what I had said about God forgiving our sins could actually be true. "How could I ever be forgiven when I've slept with so many boys that I can't even remember many of their names?" she asked us tearfully. Her life was transformed when she understood the way that Jesus lived. Let me explain.

Matthew was one of the twelve original disciples of Jesus. He records that

Jesus came from Galilee to the Jordan to be baptized by John. But John tried to deter him, saying, "I need to be baptized by you, and do you come to me?" Jesus replied, "Let it be so now; it is proper for us to do this to fulfil all righteousness." Then John consented. As soon as Jesus was baptized, he went up out of the water. At that moment heaven was opened, and he saw the Spirit of God descending like a dove and alighting on him. And a voice from heaven said, "This is my Son, whom I love; with him I am well pleased."[2]

Matthew records two things of enormous significance here. First he says that the thirty-year-old Jesus informed John the Baptist that he had never committed a single sin. When he says, *"It is proper for us to do this to fulfil all righteousness,"* he is effectively saying, *"We need to do this one last thing to give me a perfect track record of hitting God's moral target with every single action I have ever performed in my life."* The second thing is even more remarkable. Instead of striking him down as a self-deluded show-off, God the Father breaks the fourth wall by booming out a confirmation of this from heaven for the crowds. He effectively shouts out, *"Yes, the man who stands before you truly is the Son of God. I love him and can confirm that he has never committed a single action that has displeased me."*

Those words are astonishing, but they are simply the outworking of what we discovered on the first leg

2   Matthew 3:13–17. Written in c. 60 AD, Matthew's gospel is the first book of the New Testament.

of our journey of discovery. If it's true that God became a human being, it stands to reason that his One Life would be very different from our own. We were born into a human race that has the venom of sin running through its veins, poisoning everything we do. God became one of us in order to create a new human race – fully God and therefore powerful enough to resist the strong temptation of sin, yet at the same time fully human and therefore able to solve the human problem from the inside out. The Bible tells us that the words God boomed out over Jesus at his baptism he will also speak out over anyone who believes in him. Nobody ever had to teach us to do wrong because we were all born into *"the first man Adam"*, but the Bible promises that God will declare us free from sin if we become part of the new human race established by *"the last Adam"*.[3] There are now two human races, and not just one.

That's what my wife and I explained to Caroline. Her forgiveness did not depend on how much she could change her life to please God, but on the fact that somebody else had already lived a perfect life for her. God loves us so much that he faced up to the fact that we keep on sinning. The name Jesus is Hebrew for *The Lord to the Rescue*, because he knew that we could not pull ourselves out of the pit of sin. God came in person to live the life that we have failed to live so that he could present us with his own righteousness and take away our moral filth forever. Matthew was the worst kind of tax collector – one who cosied up to the

---

3   1 Corinthians 15:21–22, 45–49.

Romans in order to rob the powerless people around Lake Galilee – yet his slate was wiped clean when he accepted the great exchange that Jesus offered him. He begins his gospel by listing two prostitutes and a murderer who were forgiven in the same way. He encourages us to believe that God will forgive us too. He quotes the words of Jesus: *"It is not the healthy who need a doctor, but those who are ill... I have not come to call the righteous, but sinners."*[4]

Caroline leant back in her chair. I could tell that we were getting through. But she still had one more objection. *"How can I commit my life to Jesus when I know I'll never manage to keep up the Christian life?"* I needed to explain to her that she didn't have to. Becoming part of God's new human race isn't just about having the slate wiped clean and being given a chance to have another go at life. It carries with it a promise from God that he will fill us with the power of the Holy Spirit, the third Person of the Trinity, who comes alongside us and enables us to follow in the footsteps of Jesus instead of in those of our old sinful forefather. The Christian Gospel is an invitation to allow God to come and change us from the inside out, making our lives more and more an echo of the One Life we admire.

The Bible puts it this way:

Now that we know what we have – Jesus, this great High Priest with ready access to God – let's not let it slip through our fingers. We don't have a priest

---

4   Matthew 1:3, 5, 6; 9:9–13.

who is out of touch with our reality. He's been through weakness and testing, experienced it all – all but the sin. So let's walk right up to him and get what he is so ready to give. Take the mercy, accept the help… He's there from now to eternity to save everyone who comes to God through him, always on the job to speak up for them. So now we have a high priest who perfectly fits our needs: completely holy, uncompromised by sin, with authority extending as high as God's presence in heaven itself.[5]

Over the next few weeks, I saw Caroline's life completely transformed by a proper understanding of the life of Jesus. Because my wife and I shared his story properly, she came to see that her messed-up life could be declared perfect by trusting in the One Life that changes everything for everyone. She came to see that Jesus was more than her sinless Saviour – he was also the one who would empower her to sin less and less as she surrendered her life to him and received his Holy Spirit.

By the time Caroline left our house that evening, the words of God that boomed out over Jesus at the River Jordan had become her own. God was happy to speak over her too: *"This is my daughter, whom I love; with her I am now well pleased."*

---

5   Hebrews 4:14–16; 7:25–26, paraphrased by Eugene Peterson in *The Message*.

Dan's Story

Dan is one of my friends from Everyday Church in London

grew up in what you would call a good Christian home, but when I turned twelve I started questioning a lot of what I saw. My granddad died of cancer and I could not accept that a God who is supposed to love us could let somebody die in such a horrible way. Through this, I started to feel very detached from the young people at my church. I started hanging out with guys from school and was heavily influenced by them.

I still went to church with my parents, but I started smoking and drinking and masturbating. I was in a relationship with someone in the youth group and we ended up sleeping together. When the leaders found out about this they were not happy, to say the least, and when my parents found out, it got worse. They were very angry and disappointed with me. This led to a real low point in my life. I didn't realize it at the time but having sex that young was so emotionally damaging – not just to me but also to the girl that I had led astray. In the end, I left church altogether. I felt so judged by people. I had made a big mistake, for sure, but now I felt so rejected and unwelcome. I had had enough of people gossiping about me. I didn't want to be in a place full of such hypocrites.

I spent the next nine years wanting to have nothing to do with God. I felt so angry that I got into trouble at school. I started taking drugs, going out drinking and getting into a series of sexual relationships. This actually led to what I would now describe as a real addiction to sex. I started struggling with pornography and my complete lack of respect for women meant that I didn't treat all the girls I dated well at all. I would sleep with them and not really care if I then just moved on to another girl.

I could go on forever about some of the stuff I got up to, but I think we would run out of space in this book. I was just not in a good place and I was starting to feel really empty with life. Around that time, I met a girl named Nikki on a night out. I thought she was the prettiest girl I had ever seen. We got chatting, kissed and exchanged numbers. When she found out that my parents went to church, she started asking me what I thought about heaven and hell. I said I hadn't thought about it in a long time. She was raised a Catholic and believed that, as long as you're a good person, you will go to heaven. When she said that, I remembered some of the things I had heard from my parents and at church. I said no one is good enough. The Bible says that even the smallest sins are big in God's eyes and that we can only be forgiven through Jesus' life, death and resurrection. There I was, far from God, but preaching at my girlfriend!

Nikki was very concerned, as what I had said basically meant that she was going to hell. To be honest, I hadn't really thought about what it meant if what I had just said was true. When my parents invited her to an Alpha course at their church, I decided to go with her. When she got saved and filled with the Holy Spirit, I was hesitant, as I still had a lot of anger and hurt against the church. I decided to go back and try it, and I started feeling more and more challenged about how I was living my life. I started to pray and one day I met with God in a powerful way. I repented of the mistakes I had made and I apologized to my parents. I even felt led to seek out the leaders I had hurt in the past to say sorry. This was a massive step for me – to admit that the way I was leading my life wasn't right and that I needed to give it all to Jesus.

Nikki and I felt it wasn't right to keep on sleeping together. That had to stop. It was really hard, but God was doing an amazing work in our lives. We gave up so much but felt like we had gained everything. We eventually got engaged and married. We now head up all the kids and youth work at Everyday Church. Get the irony: I now lead the youth group that I was thrown out of! God has a real sense of humour.

My life has changed so much since saying yes to following in the footsteps of Jesus. All the emptiness I used to try and fill with sex, relationships, pornography, drugs, drinking and partying has now been filled by the love of God. I have been given such purpose and just want to share my faith with others.

If you feel like you are in a hole of sin and you can't crawl out, I plead with you to bring it all to Jesus. I prayed a random prayer, just asking if he was there and if he could ever forgive me, and I experienced such love and compassion. The people at church are not perfect and they will make mistakes. But Jesus is perfect and he is calling you.

Too Good to Be True?

Living in the modern world, it's hard not to be cynical when we are offered things for free. It's a rare day that goes by that I don't receive an email promising me a fortune if I wire some money to a Nigerian bank account or a massive pay-out if I enlist an ambulance-chasing lawyer to represent me over some long-forgotten injury.

It therefore doesn't surprise me that many people respond with cynicism to God's offer of forgiveness and personal transformation through the life of Jesus. But if you are tempted to be cynical yourself, I would encourage you to consider both the hard facts and the very unattractive alternatives to them.

The hard facts are that Jesus of Nazareth was recognized as perfect, even by his enemies. The Jewish priests and rabbis hated him so viciously that they watched him like hawks for three long years in order to find something that he said or did that denied his claim to be God. Think about how easy that would be if they were doing it to you or me. They would only have to follow me around for three hours to see that I am an imperfect human being (my wife and children say three minutes!). If you are honest, you'll admit that it would probably be the same with you. So consider this: when they put him on trial after three years, the Jewish leaders could not name a single thing that Jesus had said or done wrong. They paid false witnesses to make up accusations, but even these were so unbelievable that they decided to condemn him to death for blasphemy – for claiming to be God – the very claim they were unable to disprove! It isn't just the Christian gospel writers who tell us this. None of the early historians level a single charge of sin against him.

The Jewish leaders brought Jesus to the Roman governor, Pontius Pilate, because only he had the authority to execute him. It's interesting that they altered the charge against Jesus as they did so, recognizing that their bogus charges would never stand up in a Roman courtroom. Instead they accused him of stirring up rebellion against the emperor, a charge that no Roman governor dared be seen to ignore. After questioning him, Pontius Pilate declared three times that *"I find no basis for a charge against this man."* One of the thieves who were crucified with him agreed when he saw the way in which Jesus forgave his executioners: *"This man has done nothing wrong."* Even the leader of the squad of Roman soldiers that crucified him came to the same conclusion and regretted his actions: *"Surely this was a righteous man."*[1] Whatever your own conclusions, they therefore must take account of this phenomenon. Everyone

1   Mark 14:53–64; Luke 23:1–24, 39–41, 47.

around Jesus of Nazareth, friend or foe, was forced to recognize that he was unique among humans. He alone was innocent of sin.

Neither of the two alternatives to this conclusion is very palatable. The first is to take the approach of the *irreligious*. We live in a world that has embarked on this alternative with gusto. We fill our lives with work and television and music and newspapers and endless surfing on the internet and addictive apps and cat videos on YouTube – anything to drown out the voice of conscience that warns us on the inside that we have done wrong things and that a day of divine reckoning is coming. It works for some of the time, but it's hard work trying to pretend that a short memory is the same thing as a clear conscience. That's why we admire writers who are unafraid to address our guilty consciences and to show us a pathway to be rid of them – think of William Shakespeare's Claudius in *Hamlet*, or Victor Hugo's Valjean and Javert in *Les Misérables*, or Charles Dickens's Scrooge in *A Christmas Carol*, or J. R. R. Tolkien's Boromir in *The Lord of the Rings*. The German philosopher Immanuel Kant explains why these stories resonate with us: *"Two things fill the mind with ever new and increasing wonder and awe, the more often and more steadily we reflect on them: the starry heavens above me and the moral law within me."*[2] These writers warn us that drowning out our conscience brings us misery in this life, and even greater misery beyond the grave.

2   Kant says this in his *Critique of Practical Reason* (1788).

The second alternative is to take the approach of the *religious*. Instead of accepting that Jesus of Nazareth is in a league of his own – unique as both fully God and fully human – we search for other ways to work our own way back to God. The devotees of the world's great religions may seem very different from each other, but they have two big things in common: they work hard to earn God's favour and they end up pretty miserable, because the truth is that no amount of religious exertion can ever force God to say over us what he said freely over Jesus at his baptism in the River Jordan. No amount of Ramadan fasting, Catholic confession, Buddhist meditation, Jewish Sabbath-keeping or Hindu incense-burning can ever save us from the sin that courses through our veins. It is far too powerful to be fixed from the outside in. It can only be fixed from the inside out.

That's why Moses told the Jews that a better prophet was coming. It's why Muhammad told his followers that he was a sinner who could warn them about sin but who was powerless to save them from it. It's why the Buddha's last words to his disciples were *"Work hard to gain your own salvation."* They were all like half-trained doctors – experts at diagnosing the problem of sin, but hopeless when the time came to administer its cure.[3]

Accepting that God has come to earth is costly. It means we need to let him call the shots in our lives

---

3   Moses in the Torah in Deuteronomy 18:18; Muhammad in the Qur'an 46:9 and 48:2; the Buddha in the *Mahaparinibbana Sutta*.

instead of acting like little gods ourselves. But it is far more attractive than either of these two alternatives. Jesus alone allows us to face up to our conscience and look our moral failure squarely in the eyes. He alone offers us the serum that deals with sin's snakebite and draws its venom out of our veins. As we will see in Part 3, he alone knows how to carry our sin and punishment away.

He alone can lead us to a place where God speaks over us the words of approval that he boomed out at the River Jordan: *"You are my child, whom I love; with you I am very pleased."*

PART 3

He Died a Violent Death

He Died a Violent Death

Oe of my favourite pieces of BBC comedy is the skit in which David Mitchell and Robert Webb depict two Nazi SS officers who suddenly spot the symbolism of their uniforms. One of them asks worriedly, *"Hans, have you noticed the badges on our caps?"* His comrade looks back at him blankly, so he continues. *"The badges on our caps – have you noticed that they've got skulls on them?"* He is still met with a blank look. *"Hans, I've been thinking – do you think that we might be the baddies?"*[1]

Sometimes I think that we can be a bit like Mitchell and Webb ourselves. We wear crosses on chains around our necks. We put crosses on the spires of our churches. We tattoo crosses on our bodies. We put crosses on our gravestones and on the walls of our homes. Yet few of us stop to consider what the symbolism actually means. To first-century eyes, a cross spoke of a death so barbaric that the Roman orator Cicero urged the courts to ban it as a symbol. He argued that

---

1   *That Mitchell and Webb Look* (Season 1, Episode 1), first broadcast on BBC2 in 2006.

*The very word "cross" ought to be far removed,
not just from the bodies of Roman citizens, but also
from their thoughts, their eyes and their ears. For
being nailed to such an object is not the only thing
that is unworthy of a Roman citizen or freeman,
but so is the idea of it, the hint of it, even the mere
mention of it.[2]*

We need to understand this if we want to grasp the true significance of the One Life that changes everything for everyone. It's strange that Jesus of Nazareth is more famous for his death than for his deeds. It is even stranger that his followers chose to make the object on which he died the enduring symbol of their faith in him. To the ancient world, the cross depicted shame and disgrace and abject failure. It was far worse than a rope and gallows, far worse than a guillotine and far worse than an electric chair today. Yet the early followers of Jesus brought the cross front and centre, despising its shame and declaring that it had now become the symbol of God's great victory.

They declared that Jesus had not died by mistake. Several times during the months leading up to his crucifixion he had predicted that he was about to lay down his life of his own accord to save the world. He had referenced several ancient prophecies which predicted that the Messiah would come and die on a cross as an innocent sacrifice for all the sins that people have committed against God, and that God would look

2   Cicero said this in 63 BC in his *Pro Rabirio Perduellionis Reo* (5.16).

on the blood of his sacrifice and extend forgiveness towards anyone who believed. The disciples of Jesus told people that he had forbidden them from resisting his arrest because, *"How then would the Scriptures be fulfilled that say it must happen in this way?"*[3]

If we want to understand why Jesus is the most talked about, most written about, most sung about, most blogged about and most tweeted about person in history, we need to take time to discover why it was so important that he should die.

Jesus died on the cross to deal with *the penalty of sin*. We talked in Part 2 about the voice of conscience, nudging each of us to recognize that we have done wrong. Like the pain receptors that warn us to take our hands out of the sink because the water is scalding hot, our conscience warns us to take our sin to God and to ask for his forgiveness before those sins result in judgment. Before the death of Jesus, God had responded to this instinctive reaction by commanding people to sacrifice a sheep or a goat or a bull as a sin offering. He never quite explained how shedding the blood of an innocent animal could atone for human sin. He simply expected people to take him at his word and go to the priests to offer a sacrifice in order to receive forgiveness.

When we study the life of Jesus, we discover why those ancient sacrifices carried the power to do away with human sin. Shortly after baptizing him in the

---

3   Matthew 26:54. Jesus was referring to prophecies such as Psalm 22:16–18, Isaiah 53:5, Zechariah 12:10, and Mark 8:31, 9:31 and 10:33–34.

River Jordan, John the Baptist pointed at Jesus and prophesied, *"Look, the Lamb of God, who takes away the sin of the world!"*[4] That's why it's so significant that it was the Jewish priests who arrested Jesus and demanded his crucifixion. Without knowing what they were doing, the priests slaughtered Jesus like a sheep or goat or bull, as the ultimate sacrifice for sin.

Sometimes people ask why Jesus had to die at all. Why couldn't God have simply decided to forgive sin, without the need for any sacrifice? This fails to understand God's passionate commitment to performing justice. Every sin carries a penalty. Only a corrupt judge would attempt to sweep offences under the carpet, as our own everyday experience teaches us.

A few years ago, while reversing in a car park, I drove into the front of an expensive sports car which I hadn't seen in my rear-view mirror. It was parked up against a wall, so the force of my hitting its front bumper drove its rear bumper into the wall. I had damaged not just one end of the expensive sports car, but both. I was having a bad day! At that moment, I had a choice. I could hope that nobody had seen me and drive off quickly (in which case the owner of the sports car would have to pay for the damage) or I could leave a note of apology with my phone number on the windscreen of the car (in which case I would have to pay for the damage). But here's the thing: there was no third option of my pretending that no damage had been done. Somebody had to pay.

4   John 1:29.

I chose the second option, but the cost to me was nothing like the cost for Jesus when he died on the cross for our sins. We have already seen that he never did anything wrong. He wasn't part of the car crash of our sin, yet he chose to step into our shoes and to bear the penalty for us. The apostle Paul explains why in Romans 6:23: *"The wages of sin is death, but the gift of God is eternal life in Christ Jesus our Lord."*

Jesus also died on the cross to deal with *the pollution of sin*. When we disobey God's commands, it doesn't just make us guilty. It also makes us dirty and ashamed. It's one of the reasons why people tell lies and wear masks in front of one another. We don't want people to know who we really are. That's why it's so significant that the Romans crucified people naked, stripped and pinned up for all to see. For the six hours that it took Jesus to die, his ears were filled with the mocking laughter of the crowd. When he was crucified outside the walls of Jerusalem, the place to which people took out their rubbish and their human waste, he embraced the filth and the shame of our exclusion from God's presence so that he could bring us back to him.

The Christian writer John Stott explains:

The essence of sin is man's substituting himself for God, while the essence of salvation is God substituting himself for man. Man asserts himself against God and puts himself where only God deserves to be; God sacrifices himself for man and puts himself where only man deserves to be. Man claims prerogatives which belong to God alone; God accepts penalties which belong to man alone.[5]

Jesus also died on the cross to deal with *the power of sin*. Disobedience to God doesn't just mess up our lives. It also proves strangely addictive. Jesus taught in John 8:34–36, *"Very truly I tell you, everyone who sins is a slave to sin… If the Son sets you free, you will be free indeed."* That's why it's significant that Jesus became a prisoner for our sake. He was bound by his captors and then pinned to a cross by soldiers. He allowed his body to be subjected to their power so that he could put himself in our place. We can't free ourselves from our addiction to alcohol or pornography or angry thoughts or self-centred actions or comfort eating or pride, but Jesus died to set us free. He allowed his body to be subjected to death itself so that he could become the most powerless object in the universe – a corpse – and then lead all those who believe in his message upwards on the pathway to true liberty. In Part 4 we will see how that happens in more detail. For now, it is enough simply to point out that it's true.

The apostle Paul explains in Titus 2:11–14:

The grace of God has appeared that offers salvation to all people. It teaches us to say "No" to ungodliness and worldly passions, and to live self-controlled, upright and godly lives in this present age, while we wait for the blessed hope – the appearing of the glory of our great God and Saviour, Jesus Christ, who gave

5   John Stott in *The Cross of Christ* (1986).

*himself for us to redeem us from all wickedness and
to purify for himself a people that are his very own,
eager to do what is good.*

Christians use the cross as a symbol of victory today
because, even though it looked like a moment of defeat
and shame, it was actually the moment when the Devil
overplayed his hand. When Jesus took from us sin's
penalty, sin's pollution and sin's power, he broke sin's
stranglehold over us. He turned the table on the Devil
and set us free. Augustine of Hippo explains:

*If Christ had not been put to death, death would
not have died. The Devil was therefore conquered
by his own trophy of victory. The Devil jumped
for joy when he seduced the first man [Adam] and
threw him down to death. By seducing the first
man, he killed him, but by killing the last man, he
lost the first from his snare... The Devil jumped for
joy when Christ died, but it was through the death
of Christ that the Devil was overcome. He took the
bait in the mousetrap. He rejoiced at Christ's death,
believing himself to be the commander of death, but
what he rejoiced over was a lump of bait. The Lord's
cross was the Devil's mousetrap: the bait which
caught him was the death of the Lord.[6]*

---

6   Augustine of Hippo in c. 400 AD in his sermon "On the Ascension"
(*Sermons* 263.1).

Akhtar's Story

Akhtar is one of my friends from Everyday Church in London

I've always had something of an addictive personality. I know what I like, and when I like something I can't get enough of it. For as long as I can remember there's always been something – as a kid it was certain books, toys, TV shows and video games. As a teenager it was skateboarding and music, in a big way. I was in a band and I would only take my headphones out of my ears if I was at a concert or a festival.

As a student, my addiction became drugs. I smoked weed and hash, dabbled in speed and then graduated to ecstasy and cocaine. I loved it all and I couldn't get enough. I spent most of my waking life stoned. Each weekend felt like a mini-holiday. My friends and I would prepare for it all week long, before heading into town on a Friday night to go clubbing for the whole weekend, fuelled by a cocktail of stimulants and booze. I felt that this was what life was all about. I fully believed that I was living a great adventure. I didn't notice that I'd long stopped skateboarding or playing in a band. I didn't notice that life was slipping away from me.

By my third year at university, I was far less happy. What I now recognize as a God-given gift of leadership meant that I had led many of my friends to share my own drug-fuelled lifestyle. I didn't like how this changed and reduced them. I lost all interest in interacting with anyone in a normal way, without some thrill or risk or excitement. I knew that something had gone wrong.

That was when I began to read the Bible. Although my dad was a Muslim, I'd had an experience of God when I was nine in which I knew that God was Jesus and that Jesus was God. I had knelt on the floor in my bedroom and asked him to take my life and use me. I never went to church or did anything with it, but now that changed. The more I read, the more I knew I needed to be baptized. My testimony was simple and heartfelt: *"Jesus is Lord."* I smoked what I thought would be my last spliff and I was baptized, giving my whole life to Jesus again. I was determined now to live for God and excited about all that I would do for him. I had no idea how imprisoned I'd become by the sin that had shaped my life for so long.

As I took my first few steps into this life of service to God, I was appalled to find that I had no strength or will to do this at all. I had so powerfully trained myself to take what I wanted and to live for myself that I was utterly unable to make decisions for him or for anyone else. I quickly learned that, far from being a credit to the Lord and an asset to his team, I was useless to him, living out Romans 7:19 each day: *"For I do not do the good I want to do, but the evil I do not want to do – this I keep on doing."* Finally, admitting my failure, I returned to my old lifestyle and went deeper than ever before. I lost touch with my family and my wider group of friends. I witnessed a great deal of violence, theft, car crashes, drug dealing and abortion – all the fruit of people living for themselves, trusting in nothing more than what the moment could give them.

But God's grace was powerfully at work in my failure. I attended two Alpha courses and, even though I was still so caught up in the power of sin that I would smoke weed in the car park after each session, I was beginning to understand the greater power of God. I met a girl and we got married. Soon after, we were both baptized in the Holy Spirit – an experience that changed everything for me on two important fronts. The first was a deeper conviction of sin. Instead of making excuses, I desperately wanted to be free. The second was that God himself exercised power over the sin in my life. I found that through prayer and a heartfelt confession that I truly wanted to change – either with a church friend or on my own – my evil desires began to shrivel up and die. At one of my lowest moments, I cried out to God on the floor of my kitchen, so sorry that I couldn't keep away from sin for his sake, and I heard Jesus say to me softly: *"That is why I died."* I finally understood. There was no hope of any single one of us living well enough to live with God. God could have abandoned us to endless sin and death, but instead in love he joined us. Jesus came down, lived a perfect life and took my sin away from me when he died.

I had finally learned that the pursuit of sinful pleasure is an endless, restless cycle of chasing highs and coming down. When we surrender to God's pursuit of us, it is a source of unending peace and exhilarating love. To know him is the greatest high of all, and there really is no comedown. God is an expert craftsman, a genius, who turns even the ugliest parts of our lives into beautiful blessing for ourselves and for others. I spent so many years experiencing at first hand the deathlike power that sin holds over people. When God called me to become a social worker, and later a pastor, these lessons have left me. They have given me compassion and indelible faith that, through Jesus, anybody can be set free.

If you feel like I felt back then, rejoice in your weakness. It was for this very reason that Jesus came and died and rose again. He said that it's the sick who need a doctor, so if you're sick of your sin cry out to him. He'll come to you right now.

Too Good to Be True?

There is a brilliant scene in an episode of *The Simpsons* when Homer Simpson is about to be trampled to death by a rampaging rhinoceros. He hedges his spiritual bets as he blurts out a panicked prayer: *"I'm gonna die! Jesus, Allah, Buddha – I love you all!"*[1]

That's pretty much the culture we live in. We tend to assume that all religions are the same, so when somebody tells us that the death of Jesus on the cross can rid us of sin's penalty, cleanse us of sin's pollution and free us from sin's power, we tend to nod and smile. If that works for them, then great, but it's just one of many options that are available to the spiritual connoisseur of today. You haven't understood the significance of what happened to Jesus of Nazareth if you still think like that. You need to grasp that religion is always spelt *D-O*, whereas what Jesus did for us is spelt *D-O-N-E*.

Just before the soldiers arrived in the Garden of Gethsemane to arrest Jesus, he prayed to God the

---

1 *The Simpsons*, Season 10, Episode 15 – "Marge Simpson in: 'Screaming Yellow Honkers'" (1999).

Father for a way out so that he might not have to die. You can read about it in the account of one of the disciples who was there, in Matthew 26:36–54. Three times Jesus pleaded, *"My Father, if it is possible, may this cup be taken from me. Yet not as I will, but as you will."* After the third time of praying, he received his answer from the Father and informed his disciples that there was no other way. In this chapter, I want to help you to understand what Jesus saw that made him tell them that *"It must happen in this way."*

Jesus saw that, since religion is always spelt D-O, it is always doomed to fail. We can simply never do enough to make it up to God for our sin. It's like trying to persuade a policeman who has pulled you over for running through a red light that he should let you off because you promise to stop at every red light on the way home. It wouldn't cut ice with the policeman, and it doesn't cut ice with God. To sin is to fail to offer God the honour he is entitled to. It is to rob him of his glory, so it cannot be atoned for by a promise not to do so again. Quite apart from the fact that we can't stop sinning even if we try, that would be to expect God to treat the sinner and the sinless alike – in other words, to act unjustly and so become a sinner like us. That's why Jesus told his disciples that he had to go through with the plan to die on the cross. It was the only way that God could be just and merciful at the same time. Instead of becoming a sinner with us, he became sinless for us and traded places with us, taking what was due to us for our sin. Only God could be sinless and only a human could die on a cross, so only Jesus qualified for the role. It's because of the uniqueness of that One Life that Jesus is uniquely the Saviour of the world.

Jesus had a plethora of world religions in front of him as he knelt and prayed in agony in the Garden of Gethsemane. There was Judaism, but Jesus saw that it was spelt *D-O*. That's why he had been forced to tell even the most promising Jewish rabbis that *"no one can see the kingdom of God unless they are born again"* and *"If you do not believe that I am the one I claim to be, you will indeed die in your sins."*[2] There was also Hinduism, Buddhism, Mithraism and paganism, but Jesus could see that they were all spelt *D-O* too. There may seem to be a massive difference between the Greek king Agamemnon sacrificing his daughter to the goddess Artemis, the Hindu king Ravana amputating parts of his body to appease the god Shiva, a Pakistani Muslim fasting at Ramadan and a secular Westerner protesting that *"I'm a good person; if there is a God, he's sure to forgive me"* – but there isn't really. They all offer different manmade gifts to God in an attempt to buy forgiveness. As a result, every single one of them is doomed to fail.

What Jesus understood on his knees in the Garden of Gethsemane is that we need something other than religion, something that is spelt *D-O-N-E*. We can no more save ourselves than we can lift ourselves up by our own bootstraps, which is why God came to earth

2   John 3:3; 8:24.

as a human being to do it for us. It's why he cried out from the cross as he died that *"It is finished!"* It's why the early Christians taught that *"without the shedding of blood there is no forgiveness"*. It's why Jesus was able to turn to the thief who was crucified next to him and tell him that he was forgiven straightaway for all of his sins, even though he had no life left in which to try to make it up to God. The thief didn't need a second chance. He needed a Saviour, which is exactly what he found. Jesus turned to him with love in his eyes and reassured him, *"Truly I tell you, today you will be with me in paradise."*

That's why the message about Jesus is known as the Good News. Forgiveness isn't about what you can *do* but about what Jesus has *done*. Jesus got up from his knees and went willingly to die because there was no other way for you or me to be forgiven, which means that we can be as confident as the apostle Peter: *"Salvation is found in no one else, for there is no other name under heaven given to mankind by which we must be saved."*[3]

---

3   The Bible verses quoted in these final two paragraphs can be found in John 19:30, Hebrews 9:22, Luke 23:43 and Acts 4:12.

PART 4

He Rose from the Dead

He Rose from the Dead

Henry Ford sparked a massive revolution that is still felt in every city of the world today. If you don't believe me, here's a statistic to convince you. In 1901, the year that he founded the Henry Ford Motor Car Company, 36,000 horses were employed to pull trams in British cities. Thirteen years later, in 1914, that number had plummeted to only 900. Almost all the horses had been replaced by motor cars and buses. When Henry Ford reflected on this massive revolution, he is said to have observed with a wry smile that *"If I'd asked people what they wanted, they'd have said faster horses."*

Most of us want God to give us the equivalent of a faster horse. We want God to top up our own strength with some extra power of his own. We may not be as extreme as one of my friends, who wrecked his life by asking God to solve all his financial problems by ensuring that he won a £20,000 bet on a Premiership football match, but most of us do the same thing in miniature. We look for human solutions to our problems and then we ask God to make those solutions successful. We try to horse-trade with God, offering him prayer and worship in return for blessing the work of our hands. But God won't give us faster horses. He wants to connect us to a better power supply instead.

That's why Jesus of Nazareth is our Example as well as our Saviour. He consistently travelled on the path of human weakness because he believed that it was also the pathway towards wielding heaven's power supply. He was born in a stable (not in a palace), he was brought up in small-town Galilee (not in fashionable Jerusalem) and he trained as a common carpenter (not as a respected rabbi). As we saw in Part 3, he then allowed himself to be stripped and whipped and beaten and nailed through his hands and feet and hung on a cross for six shame-filled hours until he died. He became the weakest object in the universe – a cold and lifeless corpse – because he wasn't interested in asking God the Father to top up his human strength. He wasn't after a faster horse. He was determined to unlock the spiritual power supply of heaven.

The apostle Paul describes this revolutionary road in Philippians 2:5–8.

> *Have the same mindset as Christ Jesus: who, being in very nature God, did not consider equality with God something to be used to his own advantage; rather, he made himself nothing by taking the very nature of a servant, being made in human likeness. And being found in appearance as a man, he humbled himself by becoming obedient to death – even death on a cross!*

The key word here is humility. Jesus didn't assert his own strength and ask his Father to top it up for him. He made himself nothing, renouncing this world's power to access the power of heaven.

Many people miss this when they read about the life of Jesus of Nazareth. They fail to spot the many ways in which he emptied himself of any reliance upon human power. He was born into a family so poor that when the wine ran out at a friend's wedding he had no option of sending the disciples to the market with a wad of cash. He painted himself into a corner so that his only hope of helping his embarrassed friends was to turn water into wine through heaven's power. He continued to paint himself into that same corner by giving away any money that he received during his ministry. As a result, when he wanted to help a man who had been born blind, he had no option of paying for him to be treated by the finest doctors in the land. All he could do was to spit on the ground and put mud on the man's eyes, appealing to the God who had created the first humans out of dirt to heal the blind man out of dirt as well. As a result, the man was instantly healed.[1] Our problem is never that we are too weak for God to help us, but only ever that we are too strong. We treat prayer as a last resort instead of as our first instinct. We feel that we are doing pretty well on horse power, so we don't need God's motor car.

One of my friends made an expensive mistake.

1   An eyewitness account of these two miracles can be found in John 2:1–11 and 9:1–7.

He filled up his new car with petrol instead of diesel. Fortunately, he realized what he had done before he turned the ignition and blew his engine. He called a man to empty his fuel tank and threw the petrol away in order to fill his car with the right fuel. That's what Jesus did when he told his followers in John 5:30 that *"By myself I can do nothing."* It's what he invites us to do when he essentially says to us in Matthew 5:3, *"Lucky are those who recognize that they are spiritual beggars, for theirs is the royal power of heaven."* Yes, you heard him right. Lucky are you if your health is failing, because it stops you from relying on the fitness of your body. Lucky are you if your family and friendships are falling apart, because it stops you from relying on the strength of those around you instead of on the strength that is above you. Lucky are you if your finances are in a shambles, because it stops you from relying on money instead of on God.

Jesus refused to use brute force because he wanted to receive heaven's power. He exchanged trust in earthly horses for trust in heaven's motor car. Now he calls us to do the same.

The apostle Paul encourages us that this is the way to experience a far greater revolution than that of Henry Ford. He continues in Philippians 2:9–11: *"Therefore God exalted him to the highest place and gave him the name that is above every name, that at the name of Jesus every knee should bow, in heaven and on earth and under the earth, and every tongue acknowledge that Jesus Christ is Lord, to the glory of God the Father."*

We live in a world that talks a lot about "clean fuel". Paul warns us that none of our fuels can compare with the pure power supply that Jesus has unleashed on the earth from heaven. When he was taken down from the cross and laid as a corpse in a tomb guarded by Roman soldiers, Jesus became the weakest object in the world in the most hopeless place in the world surrounded by the greatest power in the world – and he turned this world's weakness on its head. Those who operate on this world's fuel always find it fails to go the distance. Even those who are best at it, the Julius Caesars and the Alexander the Greats of this world, find that they are unable to resist the power of death. When Jesus emptied himself of what this world calls strength, his empty corpse was able to be filled with the Holy Spirit and raised to life by God's death-defying power.

That's why the Bible summarizes the Christian Gospel as *"the good news about Jesus and the resurrection"*. It's why the book of Acts refers to the cross of Jesus three times but to the resurrection of Jesus eleven times. It's why the book of Acts speaks nine times of Jesus being killed, but sixteen times of Jesus being raised to life. It's why the apostle Paul summarizes his message as *"Jesus Christ, raised from the dead… is my gospel."*[2]

It's also why Jesus tells us that Christianity is far more than a creed. It is a decision to cut off one power supply and to start relying on another. It's why he told his disciples in Luke 9:23–24 that *"Whoever wants to be*

2   Acts 17:18; 2 Timothy 2:8.

my disciple must deny themselves and take up their cross daily and follow me. For whoever wants to save their life will lose it, but whoever loses their life for me will save it." It's why the apostle Paul tells us in Ephesians 1:18–19 that this revolution lies right at the heart of Christianity. *"I pray that the eyes of your heart may be enlightened in order that you may know… his incomparably great power for us who believe. That power is the same as the mighty strength he exerted when he raised Christ from the dead."*

So let's get really practical. If what you are reading about Jesus has made you aware of your guilt towards God, you have two choices. You can try to tackle it through this world's power, either through rebellion (which tries to drown out the voice of our conscience) or through religion (which tries to solve the problem of our sin through human effort – itself a sin). Alternatively, you can come to God in prayer right now and say to him: *Lord God, I have sinned against you and there's nothing I can do to save myself. But I believe in Jesus and in his death-and-resurrection pathway. I believe that I can be forgiven, cleansed and set free by heaven's power.* If you pray that prayer, God will forgive you and the first thing he will tell you to do is to be baptized. Your local church will help you do this. When you go underwater, it is a public proclamation that you have died and been buried with Jesus. When you come up out of the water, it is a public proclamation that you have now been raised to life by heaven's power.

Every step in the Christian life is an echo of that first step of salvation. If you are struggling to break free from a particular area of sin, come and confess to God that your own willpower and determination cannot free you. Ask him to fill you with his Holy Spirit and to change you from the inside out by his own strength instead. If you are in financial or relationship trouble, confess to God that you are powerless to climb out of the hole you are in. Tell him that you want to switch to his heavenly power.

Whatever you are facing right now, you simply cannot lose if you decide to trade in your flagging horsepower for the massive engine of God's power. You will discover how this One Life changes everything for everyone if you embrace the same power exchange as Jesus did when he died and rose from the dead. The apostle Paul promises us in 2 Corinthians 13:4 that *"He was crucified in weakness, yet he lives by God's power. Likewise, we are weak in him, yet by God's power we will live with him."*

Our problem is never that we are too weak. It is only ever that we feel too strong. So pray to God right now, as you finish this chapter. Tell him that you want to join the revolution. Tell him that you want to exchange your earthly power for heaven's power.

Malcolm's Story

Malcolm is one of my friends from Everyday Church in London

I always knew my drinking was different from that of my pals. I would always choose alcohol over a soft drink, I would always continue drinking after they had stopped and I would get irritated if they didn't drink as quickly as me.

I worked in the West End of London, where I was surrounded by alcohol. My lunchtime drinking was reasonably controlled, although I was aware that I often drank alone. After work whenever anyone was going for a drink, I would be there with them like a shot every time.

This pattern continued throughout my twenties, up until I got married and beyond. My wife Jane worked in television and had a good social life but, unlike me, had many days when she did not drink. After I got married, three events quickly conspired to accelerate my drinking into chaos.

Firstly, Jane gave up work to look after our first son. I had to accept full responsibility for providing for the family and did what I normally did under such circumstances – I ran away to the pub. Secondly, my boss at work moved to a different part of the company, leaving me feeling exposed to senior management and feeling very vulnerable. Thirdly, I had to stop playing football after dislocating my ankle and breaking my leg. This shook my confidence even more.

My drinking became more inappropriate, as my lunchtime and evening drinking accelerated. But I managed to keep down a job and I went with my family to church, so I managed to convince myself that all was fine. Then I lost my job, and Jane suggested that I move out of the family home for a while. In the confusion of my guilt and shame, I agreed. Two years were to pass before I moved back home. Telling everyone that I had controlled my drinking, it now had to take place in secret. I hid bottles of whisky in all manner of places – sometimes so creatively that even I couldn't find them! I also started drinking on my way *to* work – needing an alcohol fix in order to steady my nerves.

When I lost my next job, Jane suggested that I stop drinking, at least for a week. This would require the kind of miracle she talked about with her church friends! To my surprise, I managed to keep clean for a week. The 27th of August 1994 was arguably the most amazing day of my life, although I had no idea then that it would be the last day I would ever drink alcohol. Weeks turned into months and soon it was six months since I'd had a drink. Although my life became immeasurably better, I knew that something was still missing – perhaps the power that was setting me free. I knew that if I didn't discover the source of that power soon, I would start drinking again.

Jane and I signed up for an Alpha course at church. During the ten-week course I heard all about the One Life that changes everything for everyone. I asked somebody to pray for me, and I was filled with the Holy Spirit for the first time. I felt all my guilt and shame fall away and cried like I hadn't cried since I was a young boy. It was only later that I realized that my desire for drink had left me – totally, completely, never to return – and that the thing missing from my life all along had been God.

Well, that was over twenty years ago now – a lifetime to an alcoholic and certainly not anything I could have achieved through my own willpower. Everything about my life has changed, simply everything. Jane and I have been married for almost forty years. My two sons, now adults, are both Christians and are pastoring at the church. I have now retired at the end of a successful career. I now spend my time volunteering in a number of places, all connected with homeless guys, many of whom have similar addictions to the one I had. God has used my own dreadful experiences rather wonderfully. I am certain that none of this would have occurred if God hadn't made me sober enough to ask him to pour out his Holy Spirit into my life.

If you *think* that you might have the same problem as I did, you probably have. If you have a different type of addiction or life-controlling issue, then be honest about it and be encouraged. With God's help, you too can beat addiction and become the kind of person he designed you to be. All you have to do is reach out to him and invite him into your life. He will give you heaven's power supply – all the strength you need to overcome.

Too Good to Be True?

About two months after I surrendered my life to Jesus, I had a crisis of faith. Ironically, it was because I was trying to convert my friends. I went for a drink with my friend Crazy Paul, a Cambridge engineering student and the toughest atheist I knew, and I shared with him that I had become a Christian. I told him about the One Life who had changed everything for me, then I urged him to repent of his sins and to follow Jesus too.

What happened next is still a blur. All I can remember is that I made some very unscientific speculations about creation and Crazy Paul lived up to his name. He went bright red, lost his temper and gave me both barrels on what he thought of my newfound faith. An hour later, I beat a hasty retreat, with my mind reeling and my faith in tatters. Since then, I've received plenty of verbal attacks for my faith in Jesus, but nothing had prepared me for the first one.

The following morning, I sat in the Cambridge University History Library, trying to complete an essay, but I couldn't concentrate. My head was still spinning from the night before. Was I following a lie?

Were the last two months of walking with God just an illusion? Suddenly, I looked up and saw row after row of history books. I remembered that Jesus said in Matthew 12 that his resurrection is God's ultimate proof that the words he says are true. Christianity is not a philosophy, like Buddhism or communism or existentialism, which can be debated but never proved. It is faith in a historical event in the life of a person. Even if I couldn't argue science with Crazy Paul, if Jesus died and rose again, Christianity was true. If he didn't die and rise again, however, then I should admit I was wrong and get back to my old life of binge-drinking and sin. My history essay could wait. I had found a more important assignment. I wasn't going home until I discovered the truth about Jesus' resurrection.

Perhaps Jesus didn't die at all, or at the very least his body remained in the tomb? No, that was pretty untenable. As I scoured the books, I discovered that even the Jewish leaders and Roman soldiers who guarded the tomb of Jesus didn't attempt to deny that his body went missing. They simply told people that the disciples had stolen it. I couldn't disagree with the conclusion of the great Oxford history professor Géza Vermes:

> *When every argument has been considered*
> *and weighed, the only conclusion acceptable to*
> *the historian must be that the opinions of the*
> *orthodox, the liberal sympathizer and the critical*

*agnostic alike – and even perhaps of the disciples
themselves – are simply interpretations of the one
disconcerting fact: namely that the women who set
out to pay their last respects to Jesus found to their
consternation, not a body, but an empty tomb.*[1]

Perhaps first-century people were simply gullible, then,
and all too readily assumed that a missing body meant
a risen Christ? No, that was pretty unconvincing too.
All the evidence suggested that first-century people
were every bit as cynical as my friends and I, and I
could find no other example of a "resurrection myth"
surrounding any of the other would-be Messiahs. I
had to agree with N. T. Wright that *"They knew better.
Resurrection was not a private event. Jewish revolutionaries
whose leader had been executed by the authorities, and who
managed to escape arrest themselves, had two options: give
up the revolution, or find another leader. Claiming that the
original leader was alive again was simply not an option.
Unless, of course, he was."*[2]

Perhaps the disciples made up the whole story?
But then why make the empty tomb so central to their
message? Why state so emphatically that, unless Jesus
rose from the dead, their message was a lie?[3] Why
would they be willing to die for a claim that they
knew was a scam? Even if they did so, how would

1   Géza Vermes in his book *Jesus the Jew: A Historian's Reading of the
Gospels* (1973).
2   N. T. Wright in *Who Was Jesus?* (1992). For examples of first-century
cynicism, see Matthew 28:17, Luke 24:11, John 20:25, Acts 17:32, 26:23–24 and
1 Corinthians 15:12.
3   For example, in 1 Corinthians 15:14.

they possibly have managed to convince the world that their preposterous story was true? I had to agree with the Cambridge professor C. F. D. Moule that the emergence of the Church from a handful of Galilean peasants *"rips a great hole in history, a hole the size and shape of the resurrection… What does the secular historian propose to stop it up with?"*[4] After all, it isn't enough for us to say that a resurrection is impossible – we need to produce an alternative theory for what happened. There is nothing else that fits the size of the hole.

One theory was that somebody else had been crucified instead of Jesus. It seemed to ignore the fact that he was identified by both his friends and his enemies, and that even his own mother watched him die at the foot of the cross.

Another theory was that Jesus merely fainted and recovered later in the tomb. I had to agree with John Stott that scraping this low in the barrel actually suggested that the accounts of resurrection were true.

> Are we really to believe… that after the rigours and
> pains of trial, mockery, flogging and crucifixion he
> could survive thirty-six hours in a stone sepulchre
> with neither warmth nor food nor medical care?
> That he could then rally sufficiently to perform
> the superhuman feat of shifting the boulder which
> secured the mouth of the tomb, and this without
> disturbing the Roman guard? That then, weak and
> sickly and hungry, he could appear to the disciples

4   C. F. D. Moule in *The Phenomenon of the New Testament* (1967).

in such a way as to give them the impression that he had vanquished death? That he could go on to claim that he had died and risen, could send them into all the world and promise to be with them unto the end of time? That he could live somewhere in hiding for forty days, making occasional surprise appearances, and then finally disappear without explanation? Such credulity is more incredible than Thomas' unbelief.[5]

I never converted Crazy Paul, but in some ways he converted me. He forced me to study the history books and made me come of age, stepping into a confidence that was based on fact as well as faith, examination as well as experience.

He helped me to discover for certain that this really happened. The only question is how we will respond to it now. The apostle Paul encourages you in Romans 10:9 that *"If you declare with your mouth, 'Jesus is Lord,' and believe in your heart that **God raised him from the dead**, you will be saved."*

5   John Stott in *Basic Christianity* (1958).

PART 5

He Sat Down in Heaven

He Sat Down in Heaven

The feeling you get when you complete something memorable and you finally get to sit down to celebrate is one of the best feelings ever. Think of all the moments when you have won a football match or a game of tennis or some other sport. Think about how it felt when you emerged from the shower to meet your friends at the bar and to sit down and relish the taste of victory. Think of all the times you have thrown a party and, after all the hard work of clearing up, you have sat down to rest your tired legs and look back on an amazing evening. One of the biggest themes of the New Testament is that all those little moments of sitting down in triumph are but an echo of the greatest one in history. After Jesus rose from the dead, he appeared to his followers for forty days and then ascended back to where he had come from. He sat down in heaven.

We can tell that the writer of the New Testament letter to the Hebrews was excited about that great moment of triumph. He begins his letter with celebration:

In the past God spoke to our ancestors through the
prophets at many times and in various ways, but
in these last days he has spoken to us by his Son,
whom he appointed heir of all things, and through
whom also he made the universe. The Son is the
radiance of God's glory and the exact representation
of his being, sustaining all things by his powerful
word. After he had provided purification for sins, he
sat down at the right hand of the Majesty in heaven.
So he became as much superior to the angels as the
name he has inherited is superior to theirs. For to
which of the angels did God ever say… "Sit at my
right hand until I make your enemies a footstool for
your feet"?

Jesus sat down in heaven because his work is complete.
It was one thing for the Son of God to cry out from the
cross before he died in John 19:30 that *"It is finished!"*
and for the Spirit of God to affirm this by raising his
corpse back to life, but it was another thing for God
the Father to complete this full endorsement from the
Trinity by welcoming Jesus back into heaven with a
vivid acclamation of his victory. [1] God the Father said
to Jesus: *Son, you've done it – so pull up a chair.*

I'm sure you've noticed that you don't get many
sofas on a football pitch. Everything hangs in the
balance until the final whistle blows. Only then is it
time for the players to find a chair. God the Father
therefore told Jesus to sit down and put his feet up

1   Romans 1:4 says that *"he was declared with power to be the Son of God by his*
resurrection from the dead".

in heaven because his work of salvation is over. It's time for him to enjoy the spoils of his great victory. That's vital for you to know if you are hesitating over surrendering your life to Jesus because you think that there is no way God would ever rescue a person like you. Jesus is sitting down in heaven because he has done all it takes to save even the worst of us. If you are hesitating because you think you could never keep up following Jesus, you need to know that he is sitting down because he has done enough to empower you to follow him each day. If you are a Christian, but plagued with feelings of inadequacy and guilt, you need to know this too. Jesus is sitting down because he has been good enough for the both of you. All you need to do is to accept that it is finished.

The writer of Hebrews explains why he is so excited about Jesus' victory:

> Day after day every priest stands and performs
> his religious duties; again and again he offers the
> same sacrifices, which can never take away sins.
> But when this priest had offered for all time one
> sacrifice for sins, he sat down at the right hand of
> God, and since that time he waits for his enemies
> to be made his footstool. For by one sacrifice he
> has made perfect forever those who are being made
> holy… "Their sins and lawless acts I will remember
> no more." And where these have been forgiven,
> sacrifice for sin is no longer necessary.[2]

2   Hebrews 10:11–18, written by one of the earliest Christian leaders in c. 68 AD.

What he is saying is that Jesus sat down because the blood he shed on the cross is powerful enough to atone for every single one of your sins. The most inveterate sinner becomes every bit as much forgiven as Peter or Paul or any of the other heroes in the Bible the very moment he or she believes. It isn't about your own personal standing on any given day. It is all about Jesus sitting.

Jesus also sat down in heaven because he now has all authority and power. He didn't just sit down on a chair. He sat down on heaven's throne. Ancient thrones were fitted with a footstool made of ivory or gold, but God the Father greeted Jesus back into heaven with something better: *"Sit at my right hand until I make **your enemies** a footstool for your feet."* We have talked a few times in this book about the Devil and his demons, who hate humans because they reflect something of their Creator's glory to the world. The fact that Jesus has sat down on the throne of heaven is therefore very good news. It doesn't matter how determined they are to steal and kill and destroy. Jesus is far stronger. He will protect you if you surrender your life to him and become part of his winning team.[3]

Knowing this affects how we respond to Jesus today. If Jesus were merely a religious teacher, we might ignore his words. We might decide that our lives are happy enough without Jesus and throw this book away. Knowing that Jesus is seated on the

---

3   Take another look at Philippians 2:5–11, which we read together in Part 4 of this book. It tells us that Jesus has all authority, even over the forces of hell.

throne of heaven, however, means that that would be madness. It means that the universe revolves around him and not us. Refusing his rule will result in our being banished to hell just as surely as submitting to his rule will result in our joining him in heaven.

Jesus also sat down in heaven because he has now entrusted all his authority and power to his followers. Although many Christians mistakenly sit down and pray that Jesus will go out and save the world, Mark 16:19–20 is clear that it is meant to be the other way around. *"After the Lord Jesus had spoken to them, he was taken up into heaven and he sat at the right hand of God. Then the disciples went out and preached everywhere, and the Lord worked with them and confirmed his word by the signs that accompanied it."* Because right now there is a human being on the throne of the universe, authority and power has been conferred on every human being who believes in him.

Authority is like a police badge. It doesn't matter if you are head-and-shoulders taller than a policewoman; you still do what she says. You obey the badge and not the person who is wielding it. Power is like the policewoman's gun. If you choose to ignore her authority, she can enforce it. The fact that Jesus is seated on the throne of heaven means that he has entrusted all his followers with both his badge and his gun.

If you have surrendered your life to Jesus and been baptized as a sign that you have switched sides in the spiritual battle that rages for planet Earth, this is very good news. It means that Jesus has given you all authority over the Devil and his evil schemes. *"Then Jesus came to them and said, 'All authority in heaven and on earth has been given to me. Therefore go!'"* It also means that Jesus has plugged you into the power supply of heaven by inviting you to be filled with his Holy Spirit. *"You will receive power when the Holy Spirit comes on you; and you will be my witnesses in Jerusalem, and in all Judea and Samaria, and to the ends of the earth."*[4] The life of Jesus hasn't just freed us from the clutches of the Devil. It has given us the authority and power to go on the offensive against him. We are to go and set many other people free, because Jesus has sat down in heaven.

This is why the Christian message is referred to in the Bible as the Good News. We've misunderstood it if we see it merely as the offer of forgiveness, because forgiveness is simply how we start the journey. Forgiveness reconciles us to God as our Father so that we can become part of his family business in the world, pushing back the work of the Devil in order to save many lives. The Christian message isn't about escaping from the pain of this world and being carried off to heaven. It is about bringing heaven down to this world in order to chase some of the pain away.

Where you see hurt and pain around you, pray as Jesus commanded you: *"Let your kingdom come."* Where you see the self-destructiveness of sin, pray again: *"Let*

---

4   Matthew 28:18–20; Acts 1:8. Note the way that Acts 2:33–35 links the gift of the Holy Spirit to the fact that Jesus has sat down on the throne of heaven.

your kingdom come." Where you see sickness and self-harm and the work of demons in the world, assert your authority and your God-given power. Keep on praying *"Let your kingdom come."*[5] Don't rule yourself out of the action. It isn't about how powerful you are tempted to feel you are. It is all about the fact that Jesus is sitting on the throne of heaven.

This is what the early Christians discovered was true, and it was how they rocked the world. They became so well known for their miracles and for delivering people from demons that Tertullian told the young men of the Roman Empire that they ought to become Christians, because it was much more fun fighting for the cause of Christ in the world than it was to be a mere spectator at one of the gladiatorial games![6] Their miracles became so widespread that Origen was able to say:

> *We may observe that Christians do this... merely by prayer and by simple commands which the plainest person can use because, for the most part, it is uneducated people who perform this work... It does not require the power and wisdom of those who are good at arguing or who are most educated in matters of faith.*[7]

5   You will receive practical training in how to do this from your church leaders. If you are still stuck, I take people through what this means in much more detail in my book *Straight to the Heart of Acts* (2010).

6   Writing in c. 200 AD, this is Tertullian's concluding argument in his treatise *On the Public Shows*.

7   Origen wrote this in c. 248 AD in his *Against Celsus* (7.4).

Wielding the power and authority of heaven isn't the preserve of an elite few believers. It is bread-and-butter Christianity for anybody who believes. All of this has been made possible because Jesus has sat down in heaven.

Adrian's Story

Adrian is one of my friends from Everyday Church in London

I grew up as the headmaster's son at one of Britain's leading public schools. I had a privileged life, surrounded by people who had almost everything they could have wanted. Anything was possible and I became super-ambitious and very confident.

My picture of Christianity was of a church that was half empty, mainly for old people. When I occasionally visited churches, the mood was sombre or even sad. This was epitomized by morose pictures of Jesus bleeding and dying. There was nothing about church I found appealing.

I was having fun exploring a myriad of opportunities and excitements that were available to me. I loved the camaraderie among my group of friends, with parties every weekend. Then one of my friends suddenly invited us all to the evening service at her church. I wondered: *"What kind of church would you possibly want to go to?"* We were so curious that we all said yes. The following Sunday, twenty of us turned up to see what our friend had got into.

I met people there who were excited about "knowing God personally". They had a living, vital, dynamic faith, and although I found this slightly alarming I liked the music and the socializing. In conversation, these people did not fit my stereotype of being needy or gullible.

After several visits to this church, I decided to open a Bible. I wanted to make sure that no one saw me. I was embarrassed at the thought that anyone would think I'd gone soft or weird, so I hid in the back of a red Volkswagen car. In the bit I read, Jesus was saying some outrageous things, haranguing the Pharisees. He was a million miles away from "the gentle Jesus meek and mild" I'd expected to find. Those ten minutes were enough to make me realize that there was a good chance that almost everything I'd previously thought about Christianity was wrong.

By now, only a handful of my friends were still going to church every week, but something was happening to me. During the singing, some of my hardness of heart was being melted. Worshipping

God was becoming a strangely pleasurable pastime. There was no change, however, in my behaviour or lifestyle.

Then I was directly challenged in a personal conversation with the church leader as I left the building. He cornered me and questioned me intently. I told him that I thought I was a Christian, by which I meant that I was one of the good guys. I'd not murdered anyone, I believed in God and I was British. What more could I need?! He used a vivid illustration to show me that however good I thought I was, I wasn't pure enough for a perfect heaven.

Although I lied to him and told him I didn't understand his illustration, deep down I had always been aware that I was a massively selfish person. Looking back now, I think that during those sung worship times God was invisibly doing something to connect my emotions to the reality of my selfishness. And now, the church leader had told me bluntly that I wasn't going to go to heaven, that I wasn't a Christian at all. Although I found this offensive, for years previously I'd been 100 per cent certain that I was a disgracefully selfish person and I could give you a thousand examples. I was now becoming aware that the so-called "problem of sin" was a personal problem I had.

Then someone explained how, when Jesus died on the cross, he was taking the penalty for my sin as a substitute. Suddenly it all made sense. I understood why Jesus' death was relevant. When I decided to follow Jesus, I genuinely felt like I'd been born again. There was a new peace and an overflowing joy that hadn't been there before. I was truly amazed that I'd been forgiven. Jesus had paid the price for my selfishness! The barrier between me and God had been removed as a result. I was entering a brand-new life. I was thrilled to think I had a real connection to the living God.

Later, as a national newspaper journalist and BBC Radio and TV presenter, I was trained to be cynical and to doubt and disbelieve everything and everyone. We were taught how to tear apart every source that claimed to be telling the truth. Yet I became convinced by the historical evidence that the New Testament is trustworthy and that Jesus lived and died and physically rose from the dead, and that he then ascended to heaven.

Now I've given up my journalism career to spend all my time seeking to share the reality of God's love through Jesus with people. One aspect of this is that I've found that many injured, sick or ill people are healed when I pray for them in Jesus' name. I am a naturally sceptical person, so when meeting them again a year later, I've asked them for medical documents that show they really had the condition and that a health professional has really confirmed that they are healed. Some of these healings are difficult to explain on a medical basis, such as instant recovery of sight in the visually impaired or someone born deaf in one ear who can suddenly hear normally.

In summary, I've found that the attractive thing in Christianity is a person. It's the person of Jesus Christ – who he is and the authority he bears. Discovering the love of God for me and for others in Jesus has quite simply been the most exciting thing that has ever happened to me.

Too Good to Be True?

When Jesus of Nazareth ascended to heaven in May 30 AD, he left behind only 120 faithful followers. They were a ragtag assortment of fishermen, farmers and former prostitutes and scoundrels. The chances of their faith surviving even for the next few months were next to nil, and yet it did more than simply survive. It spread to every town and city in every corner of the world.

The early Christians knew that they were witnessing a miracle. They also knew that at the heart of all their progress lay the authority and power that Jesus had entrusted to them when he sat down in heaven and sent them out into the world. The apostle Paul gives a disarmingly simple explanation for why the Christian message conquered hearts and minds across the Roman Empire: *"I will not venture to speak of anything except what Christ has accomplished through me in leading the Gentiles to obey God by what I have said and done – by the power of signs and wonders, through the power of the Spirit of God."*[1]

---

1   Paul wrote this in c. 57 AD in Romans 15:18–19.

He was right. The Christian message spread like wildfire through the streets of Jerusalem and Judea because the apostles healed crowds of people in Jesus' name. It spread through Samaria and Cyprus and modern-day Turkey because they performed similar miracles in the pagan cities too. It spread through Greece and Malta and Italy in the same way. The followers of Jesus declared that he had conquered sin and the Devil, and then they proved it by healing illnesses and by driving out demons.[2]

People nowadays tend to be cynical about the vast array of healing stories from the first three centuries AD. Ramsay MacMullen, history professor at Yale University, warns us not to be:

> *Driving all competition from the field head-on was crucial. The world, after all, held many dozens and hundreds of gods. Choice was open to everybody. It could thus be only a most exceptional force that would actually displace alternatives and compel allegiance; it could be only the most probative demonstrations that would work. We should therefore assign as much weight to this, the chief instrument of conversion, as the best, earliest reporters do.*

He likens the early Christians to Clint Eastwood facing down a crooked sheriff at the end of a Western movie:

2   Acts 2:43; 3:1–10; 5:12–16; 6:8; 8:4–8; 9:10–19, 32–42; 13:4–12; 14:3, 8–10; 16:16–18; 19:11–12; 28:7–10.

The manhandling of demons — humiliating them,
making them howl, beg for mercy, tell their secrets,
and depart in a hurry — served a purpose quite
essential to the Christian definition of monotheism:
it made physically (or dramatically) visible the
superiority of the Christian's patron Power over
all others. One and only one was God. The rest
were daimones demonstrably, and therefore already
familiar to the audience as nasty, lower powers that
no one would want to worship anyway.[3]

This remained a primary feature of Christianity for almost 300 years. Early writers such as Justin Martyr, Irenaeus, Tertullian and Origen speak about miracles as commonplace affairs. After the conversion of the Roman emperor in 312 AD, the accounts begin to dwindle, as the Christians stopped relying on the authority and power of heaven and started to plant churches and make converts through the authority and power of Rome instead. Nevertheless, whenever we read about seasons of rapid expansion for the Christian faith, we find that they were sparked by a rediscovery of what it means for us to say that Jesus has sat down on the throne of heaven.

There is Saint Patrick, who converted the nation of Ireland in a single generation through a series of astonishing miracles that exposed the druids as charlatans. There is Bernard of Clairvaux, who planted 343 monasteries in the twelfth century through his

3   Ramsay MacMullen in *Christianizing the Roman Empire, AD 100–400* (1984).

healing miracles. In a single day, he healed nine blind people, ten deaf mutes and eighteen people who were paralysed. There is Francis of Assisi, who healed a crippled boy in Toscanella, a paralysed man in Narni and a leper he met on the road in Umbria. D. A. Carson, a theologian known for his healthy scepticism, warns us that *"There is enough evidence that some form of 'charismatic' gifts continued sporadically across the centuries of church history that it is futile to insist on doctrinaire grounds that every report is spurious or the fruit of demonic activity or psychological aberration."*[4]

There is Martin Luther, the sixteenth-century reformer, who taught people that *"If the physicians are at a loss to find a remedy… this must be counteracted by the power of Christ and with the prayer of faith. This is what we do."* There is John Wesley, the eighteenth-century founder of Methodism, who reflects on the many miraculous healings in his diary and says, *"I wait to hear who will either disprove this fact, or philosophically account for it."*[5] There are the Pentecostal preachers of the twentieth century, or even my friend Adrian, who just shared with you his story. Although we may not see as many miracles among our own friends as we might like to, we mustn't miss the fact that healing is still happening everywhere.

If you are unsure whether or not you believe all that you have read in this book about the One Life of Jesus, these miracles are meant to help you. Jesus turns

4   D. A. Carson in *Showing the Spirit* (1987).

5   Luther in a letter to Severin Schulze on 1st June 1545. Wesley in his Journal on 25th December 1742.

to you in John 10:37–38 and challenges you: *"Do not believe me unless I do what my Father does. But if I do it, even though you do not believe me, believe the miracles, that you may know and understand that the Father is in me, and I in the Father."*

And if you have already surrendered your life to Jesus, understand that this is part of what it means. It isn't just about having your sins forgiven. It's about the fact that Jesus has sat down in heaven and sent you out into the world to demonstrate to others that his One Life changes everything for everyone. Don't miss what Peter Brown, history professor at Princeton University, concludes about the mission that Jesus has given you:

> *However many sound social and cultural reasons the historian may find for the expansion of the Christian church, the fact remains that in all Christian literature from the New Testament onwards, the Christian missionaries advanced principally by revealing the bankruptcy of men's invisible enemies, the demons, through exorcisms and miracles of healing.*[6]

---

6   Peter Brown in *The World of Late Antiquity* (1971).

PART 6

He Is Coming Back

He Is Coming Back

A few years ago, I went to the funeral of a 95-year-old woman. One of her relatives on the front row cried out in loud wails of anguished grief throughout the service. A small part of me found it very strange. The woman had had a good innings. She hadn't died young or painfully or tragically. If our culture is right that life is all about having fun and being happy, then her life had been a success story. Her relatives ought to have been celebrating her death instead of lamenting it with distraught tears.

But deep down I understood perfectly why her relative was grieving. He wasn't just weeping for his own loss, but for her loss too. It doesn't matter how long we live or how much we have managed to cram our lives with happy moments, we still feel the acute injustice of death when it all comes to an end. We sense that death is an imposter, an intruder who steals what ought not to be his. The nineteenth-century essayist William Hazlitt notes how significant this is: *"Man is the only animal that laughs and weeps; for he is the only animal that is struck with the difference between what things are, and what they ought to be."*[1]

William Hazlitt points out that this is not merely the case when we are confronted with death. It is also true whenever we encounter injustice. We live in the only world that we have ever known, and yet we rage against the way we find it. It is as if we know deep down that we were created for a better world than this.

C. S. Lewis reflects that

Creatures are not born with desires unless satisfaction for those desires exists. A baby feels hunger: well, there is such a thing as food. A duckling wants to swim: well, there is such a thing as water. Men feel sexual desire: well, there is such a thing as sex. If I find in myself a desire which no experience in this world can satisfy, the most probable explanation is that I was made for another world... Earthly pleasures were never meant to satisfy it, but only to arouse it, to suggest the real thing. If that is so, I must take care, on the one hand, never to despise, or be unthankful for, these earthly blessings, and on the other, never to mistake them for the something else of which they are only a kind of copy, or echo, or mirage. I must keep alive in myself the desire for my true country, which I shall not find till after death; I must never let it get snowed under or turned aside; I must make it the main object of life to press on to that other country and to help others to do the same.[2]

1   William Hazlitt in his essay *On Wit and Humour* (1818).
2   C. S. Lewis in his book *Mere Christianity* (1952).

That's why it is such good news for us that Jesus is coming back from heaven. It means that the world that we long for is not a figment of our own imagination. It is one of the greatest clues God has placed inside each one of us that the One Life of Jesus will one day change everything for everyone. He will re-create the world as it was always meant to be.

There are several mistakes that we can make here. The first is to imagine that the idea of Jesus returning from heaven is simply a fairy story. The apostle Peter warns us not to mistake his delay for deliberation:

> You must understand that in the last days scoffers will come, scoffing and following their own evil desires. They will say, "Where is this 'coming' he promised?"… But do not forget this one thing, dear friends: with the Lord a day is like a thousand years, and a thousand years are like a day. The Lord is not slow in keeping his promise, as some understand slowness. Instead he is patient with you, not wanting anyone to perish, but everyone to come to repentance. But the day of the Lord will come like a thief. The heavens will disappear with a roar; the elements will be destroyed by fire, and the earth and everything done in it will be laid bare.[3]

Jesus has only delayed coming back from heaven in order to give people like you and me enough time to surrender our lives willingly to him before the curtain falls.

3   2 Peter 3:3–10.

The second mistake is to imagine that the return of Jesus will be similar to his arrival in Bethlehem. It's easy to make that mistake as an unbeliever, persuading yourself that Jesus will be weak and unassertive on the Final Day, sweeping people's sin under the carpet instead of confronting them with his resurrection power. It's also easy to make that mistake as a believer, like the woman who said to me that she couldn't wait to run straight up to Jesus to give him a kiss when he returns. The Bible warns us that it isn't going to be like that. John was one of the twelve disciples and knew Jesus so well that he leaned back on his chest when he was tired at mealtimes, yet even he fainted with fear when he saw Jesus in his ascended glory at the start of the book of Revelation. *"His face was like the sun shining in all its brilliance. When I saw him, I fell at his feet as though dead."* The Bible warns us that nobody will be able to trifle with the baby of Bethlehem on that day. *"As lightning that comes from the east is visible even in the west, so will be the coming of the Son of Man… All the peoples of the earth will mourn when they see the Son of Man coming on the clouds of heaven, with power and great glory."*[4]

The third mistake is for us to imagine that the return of Jesus from heaven will spell destruction for the earth. This is based on a misunderstanding of Peter's words above. Jesus will only destroy the world as we know it in the same way that a landscape gardener rotavates a piece of wasteland in order to turn it into

4   Revelation 1:16–17; Matthew 24:27–31.

a magnificent garden. That's why he described his Second Coming to his disciples as *"the renewal of all things"*, and it's why they themselves described it as the moment *"for God to restore everything, as he promised long ago through his holy prophets"*.[5] God created this world perfect but we have ruined it through sin. Jesus has therefore promised to root out sin completely from the earth so that he can re-create the heavens and the earth as they were always intended to be. We grieve at funerals and we rage against injustice because God has placed in us an instinctive belief that one day this world will be restored into a paradise forever.[6]

The fourth mistake is to assume that the return of Jesus will be good news for us all. God warns in Amos 5:18 that this shows naivety about the seriousness of sin: *"Woe to you who long for the day of the Lord! Why do you long for the day of the Lord? That day will be darkness, not light."* It is brilliant news that Jesus is radically committed to rooting out sin from the earth – but only if we have turned away from sin ourselves! Otherwise we are part of the problem he is coming back to rectify. The Bible prophesies that Jesus will throw the Devil and his demons into hell so that they can trouble the earth no more – *"The devil, who deceived them, was thrown into the lake of burning sulphur, where the beast and the false prophet had been thrown. They will be tormented day and night for ever and ever"* – but it also tells us that

5   Matthew 19:28; Acts 3:21.
6   The Bible says that heaven is where God's people go when they die now. When Jesus returns, he will fuse the new heavens and new earth together into one place where God and his people will live together forever.

God will deal the same way with any human who has resisted his claim to be their Lord and who has therefore sided with the Devil in his rebellion:

> *Those who are victorious will inherit all this, and I will be their God and they will be my children. But the cowardly, the unbelieving, the vile, the murderers, the sexually immoral, those who practise magic arts, the idolaters and all liars – they will be consigned to the fiery lake of burning sulphur. This is the second death.*[7]

You should find this very sobering if you have reached the final part of this book without yet deciding to confess your sins to God and to surrender your life to Jesus as your new Master. It tells you that the stakes are far higher than you imagine. Jesus is not merely offering you a better life or a pathway to greater happiness, even if those things are likely to come as side effects. He is offering you what the Bible calls *salvation*. He is offering to forgive you for your rebellion against God and to cleanse you so thoroughly from sin that when he returns you will not be part of the problem. You will be part of the people that he loves so fervently that the Bible refers to his Second Coming as the great wedding day between Jesus the Bridegroom and the Church his Bride.

That's why I've been encouraging you to treat the One Life of Jesus as amazingly good news. If you admit your sin, put your faith in Jesus and surrender

7   Revelation 20:10; 21:7–8.

your life to him, the Bible says that God the Father will unite your own life with that of his Son. He will consider you sinless, because Jesus switched places with you on the cross. He will consider you to be part of his new creation, because your faith in Jesus means that you have been united with him in his death and burial and resurrection. That's what got the apostle Paul so excited in his New Testament letters:

We know that the one who raised the Lord Jesus from the dead will also raise us with Jesus and present us with you to himself... Therefore we do not lose heart. Though outwardly we are wasting away, yet inwardly we are being renewed day by day. For our light and momentary troubles are achieving for us an eternal glory that far outweighs them all. So we fix our eyes not on what is seen, but on what is unseen, since what is seen is temporary, but what is unseen is eternal.[8]

You should want all that you have read in this book to be true, because it is seriously good news for us. Without Jesus, this world holds all the heaven we will ever experience. But with Jesus, this world holds all the hell we will ever experience. The difference is enormous. The paradise that Adam lost has been won back for us by Jesus. The world that was ruined by sin will be re-created by Jesus on the day that he returns. Because he became fully human he was able to undo the work of Adam. Because he remained fully God he

8   2 Corinthians 4:14–18.

is able to redo the work of creation. That's why his One Life changes everything for everyone.

What a promise, what a hope, what a Saviour and what an urgent choice lies before each one of us. Jesus has held back the Final Day to grant us time to receive him as our Lord, but one day all the waiting will suddenly end. He is coming back from heaven.

Yvonne's Story

Yvonne is one of my friends from Everyday Church in London

On 25th May 2014, the first case of Ebola was recorded in Sierra Leone. In the weeks that followed, the disease spread like wildfire and on 30th July 2014 the government of Sierra Leone declared a national state of emergency. All schools and markets were closed and public gatherings were banned. Within the space of eight weeks, the number of cases had climbed to over 500 and there were about 100 new cases being recorded weekly. Businesses closed and hysteria and fear spread, as the health system was overwhelmed by the scale of the unfolding epidemic.

Although I am originally from Sierra Leone, I watched the crisis developing on my television in the safety of my home in London. To say that my heart was burdened would be an understatement. I made desperate calls to family and friends, enquiring about their safety and trying to understand what was actually happening on the ground. On Saturday 9th August, I woke up crying for my country. For the next three hours I wept before God, pleading for him to intervene and save my people. I felt burdened to act but did not know what to do. That morning, as I cried out to the Lord, I insisted that the horror unfolding in Sierra Leone was not in keeping with God's original design for creation. This was not what his Kingdom looked like and I was turning to him to save us.

The disease continued to spread and by September 2014 there were over 1,000 confirmed cases in Sierra Leone. There were insufficient beds to treat the sick, dead bodies were being left on the streets and the economy was collapsing, as many countries shut their borders and Sierra Leone became increasingly isolated. When the British government committed to provide 700 treatment beds, to deploy soldiers and to support NHS staff who wanted to travel to Sierra Leone to work in Ebola treatment centres, I helped lead a recruitment drive and held road shows in London, Manchester and Birmingham. The road shows received significant media coverage. Momentum grew and volunteers began to come forward to support the response efforts in Sierra Leone.

By October 2014, I knew that I needed to be in Sierra Leone. The disease was spreading even faster now and there were over 400 new confirmed cases every week. I travelled to Sierra Leone in November as part of the UK Medical Team. God led and guided me as I began to contribute quietly and pray that his Kingdom would come. At the start of January, I was asked to become Director of Planning at the National Ebola Response Centre! It was surreal. I felt completely out of my depth – I have come to realize that this is how God works.

On Saturday 7th November 2015, after recording zero new cases for forty-two consecutive days, the Ebola outbreak in Sierra Leone was declared over by the World Health Organization. I returned to London exactly one year after I left for Sierra Leone. Those twelve months were without question the most challenging and intense months of my life. I saw such incredible suffering, fear and loss but also witnessed amazing courage, care and compassion from ordinary people. Heroes emerged in the most difficult of circumstances, demonstrating the heart of God.

I have been reminded that God can use anyone to be his hands and feet. I had no prior experience or epidemiological training; no medical background. In recognition of my contribution to ending the Ebola outbreak in Sierra Leone, I was awarded an OBE in the Queen's 2016 New Year's Honours List. I also received an Ebola Gold Award from the President of Sierra Leone in December 2015.

The burden I felt for my nation intensified during the Ebola outbreak, as I recognized that so much of the suffering had been exacerbated by systemic failures of governance. I found myself praying again, asking God to lead me. On 14th December 2015, God spoke to me and I recorded the words in my prayer journal: *"I have called you to build the economy and to declare my Kingdom come."* Exactly one week later, I was invited by the President of Sierra Leone to serve as one of the leaders in his post-Ebola economic recovery plan for Sierra Leone. The task is daunting. The challenge of playing a strategic role in seeking to turn around a country's economy and to improve governance at the same time is enormous, but I have confidence that this is God's plan not mine, that he will allow his power to flow through me to deliver his purposes.

If you are in a difficult situation and cannot see how it can change, I want to encourage you to look outside of yourself, to recognize that God is not limited by our limitations. He made the world, he has done what it took to redeem it, and he is coming back to restore it forever. In the meantime, he can truly make his Kingdom come through you and me. Start praying like I did: *"Father, let your Kingdom come."* None of us have the first idea of all that God is able to do.

Too Good to Be True?

There is a famous joke about a man who was caught in a terrible storm. The rain came down so heavily that a policeman knocked on his door and warned him that the nearby river was about to burst its banks, but the man refused the offer of a ride to safety in the police car. *"I have been praying,"* he explained. *"God will save me."*

An hour later, the river had burst its banks and the lower floor of the man's house had been flooded. A fire engine pulled up in the driveway and its team of firemen offered to rescue him. *"I have been praying,"* he explained again. *"God will save me."*

Two hours later, the man had been forced to retreat upstairs and the upper floor of his house was quickly getting flooded too. When a speedboat pulled up alongside his top-floor window, he gave the same refusal as he climbed onto the rooftop. When a coast guard helicopter lowered down a ladder to him as he clung to the chimney in the dying light of day, he refused help yet again. *"Don't worry about me. I have been praying. I know that God will save me."*

Shortly after the helicopter disappeared into

the distance, the man's house disappeared under the rising waters and he was drowned. Waking up in heaven, he was furious. *"I trusted you, God!"* he fumed. *"I believed that you would save me. Why didn't you help me?!"*

God looked at him and shrugged his shoulders in disbelief. *"What do you mean? I sent you a police car, a fire engine, a speedboat and a helicopter…"*

You have now reached the end of this short book about the One Life of Jesus. Watch out that you are not like the man in that joke. God has given you all the proof you need to believe in him in these pages. The question is whether your eyes and ears are open to what he is saying and whether or not you are willing to step on board.

In Part 1 of this book, we looked at what is known as the Incarnation, the moment when God became one of us, a flesh-and-blood human being. We noted that none of the historians of the period deny the facts about the life of Jesus. The Jewish, Roman and Christian writers all agree that a remarkable religious teacher arose in first-century Israel.

In Part 2, we looked at the uniquely sinless life that Jesus lived among us. We noted that even his greatest enemies were unable to prove that he had ever put a foot wrong. That sets him apart from even the greatest religious leaders of history. He didn't merely point the way to God. He lived the kind of holy life that people need to live if they want to know God in his purity without being destroyed. We noted that he then gave his own perfect track record to us and carried away our impurity when he died on the cross. We discovered that he is our substitute, the sinless sacrifice for our sin.

In Part 3, we looked at the violent death of Jesus. We discovered the uniqueness of his self-sacrifice for us. It isn't just that he is better than the founders of the world's great religions. It's that he did something for us that none of them even claimed to do. They all offer flawed hopes of earning our way back into God's good books ourselves, whereas Jesus gives us everything for free. We noted Romans 6:23 together: *"The wages of sin is death, but the gift of God is eternal life in Christ Jesus our Lord."*

In Part 4, we looked at the resurrection of Jesus. We looked at the various ways in which people interpret the historical facts and we noted that, however difficult it might be to believe in the bodily resurrection of the corpse of Jesus, it is nowhere near as unlikely as the alternatives. We saw that this lies at the heart of why this One Life changes everything for everyone. We heard God knocking on our door with his offer of salvation in Romans 10:9: *"If you declare with your mouth, 'Jesus is Lord,' and believe in your heart that God raised him from the dead, you will be saved."*

In Part 5, we looked at the authority and power that Jesus now wields from his throne in heaven. We discussed the importance of miracles as a stepping stone to belief, and we conducted a quick overview of Church history to see that such signs and wonders have attested to the truth of the Christian message in every age.

In Part 6, we discovered how high the stakes are in the way we respond to Jesus. We looked at his promise to return from heaven to end world history as we know it and to remake the universe as it was always intended to be. We looked at the fact that he will merge the new heavens and the new earth together in order to create a paradise in which God will dwell forever with the people he has saved. But we also looked at the price tag for paradise. We reflected on what it means for Jesus to rid the earth of sin and rebellion against God. It doesn't just mean the eternal destruction of the Devil and his demons in hell. It also means the eternal destruction of every man and woman whose actions side with them.

So if you have not yet knelt down and repented of your sin, I want to invite you to respond to the rescue package that God has sent you in the form of his own Son. It won't be good enough for you to tell Jesus on the Final Day that you were waiting for another book, another miracle or another opportunity to put your faith in him. He will look at you with eyes of sadness, and you will find that the joke about the man and the flood waters is the tragic story of your one life. It doesn't have to be that way. As you end this book, you can make this prayer your own:

Lord God, I have sinned. I need a Saviour. Thank you so much that you have given me one in your own Son. I believe that Jesus of Nazareth is the Son of God. I believe that he lived the perfect life for me and died a violent death for me. I believe he rose from the dead and has now sat down in heaven for me. I believe that he is coming back for me so that I can be with you forever. I therefore repent of my sins and I promise to turn away from them. I declare that the risen Lord Jesus is now my Master. My old life is over. I am living for you now, God my Father. Amen.

If you have just prayed that prayer for the first time, well done. The One Life that changes everything for everyone has now changed everything very practically for you. You are now part of the same team as the many believers who are finishing this book alongside you. He therefore gives you the same calling that he gives to them in Matthew 10:27–39:

What I tell you in the dark, speak in the daylight; what is whispered in your ear, proclaim from the roofs. Do not be afraid of those who kill the body but cannot kill the soul. Rather, be afraid of the One who can destroy both soul and body in hell… Whoever does not take up their cross and follow me is not worthy of me. Whoever finds their life will lose it, and whoever loses their life for my sake will find it.

You've only got one life, so use it to enjoy what Jesus has whispered to you through this book and to pass those things on to others who need to know. You will never regret saying yes to Jesus and to finding your place among the people he has saved.

Conclusion: One Life

"People willingly believe what they wish to be true." That's what Julius Caesar claimed, and 2,000 years of history suggests that it is true.[1]

It is true in a bad sense. When many people discover that their culture is fatally mistaken in the way it views the One Life of Jesus, they quickly cover up the facts in order not to find themselves at odds with those who live around them. Warren Buffet warns that such an attitude is disastrous on Wall Street: *"What the human being is best at doing is interpreting all new information so that their prior conclusions remain intact."* It is even more disastrous when it comes to how we each invest the one life God has given us.

Fortunately, though, it is also true in a good sense. Who wouldn't wish to believe that our lives on this tiny planet are so significant that God became one of us in order to save us? Who wouldn't wish to believe that Jesus has lived the sinless life we failed to live and died the violent death we deserve to die? Who wouldn't wish to believe that there is a perfect human

---

1   Caesar says this in his *Gallic Wars* (3.18).

being sitting at the controls of the universe in heaven, or that he is coming back to re-create the paradise that deep down we are all longing for? Who wouldn't want to invest their own life in following the One Life that changes everything for everyone? As we finish, I therefore want to give you some final help to do so.

Following Jesus begins by finding out more about the way he lived and what he wants for our lives. The best way to do that is to read the four gospel accounts of his life in the Bible. I have already introduced you to **Matthew**, **Mark**, **Luke** and **John** in this short book about Jesus. Your next step is to find a Bible, either at a bookshop or online, and to read these four biographies by his friends. If you would like some help to understand the meaning of those gospels, I have written a series of **"Straight to the Heart"** commentaries which act as a chapter-by-chapter tour guide through the pages of each book of the Bible. Take a look at **www.philmoorebooks.com**.

Following Jesus also means talking to him and beginning a friendship with him. The way I do that personally is to read a chapter of the Bible with a notebook in my hand and to write down anything that I feel God is saying to me through the verses that I read on a particular day. I use these notes as a prayer list that fuels my conversations with Jesus after I have finished reading. It's pretty simple, really. He speaks and we respond. We read the Bible and then we pray. These little conversations produce a deep friendship with Jesus if we devote ourselves to it every day. I explain a little more about this in four short videos that you can watch at **www.everyday.org.uk/new**.

Following Jesus also means finding a church where you can connect with other people who are on the same journey as you. This isn't just a good idea; it's one of the things that Jesus commands his followers to do. The church I lead in London has several online congregations at **www.everyday.online**, but there is probably a great church in your home town too. Pay it a visit. Your church leaders will help you to get to know Jesus better, and they will also help you to be baptized in water and filled with the Holy Spirit.

We began this book by noting that Jesus Christ is the most thought about, talked about, written about, sung about, blogged about and tweeted about person in history. I have tried to help you to get to know him and to make a choice to join his team. You will never regret deciding to say yes to him as your Master, as your Lord and as your God.

You will never regret surrendering your one life to the One Life that changes everything for everyone.

JESUS, RIGHT WHERE YOU WANT HIM
Your biggest questions. His honest answers

Phil Moore

Written in a punchy and easy-to-read style, this is a starting point for those who want to address key issues and get answers to the big questions, such as: Hasn't religion been the cause of appalling violence? Aren't Christians a bunch of hypocrites? And isn't the Bible full of myths and contraditions?

ISBN 978 0 85721 677 9

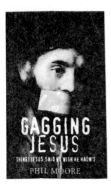

GAGGING JESUS
Things Jesus Said We Wish He Hadn't

Phil Moore

If you ever suspected that Jesus wasn't crucified for acting like a polite vicar in a pair of socks and sandals, then this book is for you. Fasten your seatbelt and get ready to discover the real Jesus in all his outrageous, ungagged glory.

ISBN 978 0 85721 453 9

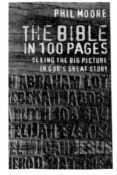

THE BIBLE IN 100 PAGES
Seeing the Big Picture in God's Great Story

Phil Moore

Most people want to discover the message of the Bible but they find it hard to see the wood for the trees. That's why this book is so helpful. It will help you to see the big picture in God's great story. It will help you to read the entire Bible with fresh eyes.

ISBN 978 0 85721 551 2